MACMILLAN MODERN NOVELISTS

General Editor: Norman Page

MACMILLAN MODERN NOVELISTS

Published titles

SAUL BELLOW   Peter Hyland
ALBERT CAMUS   Philip Thody
FYODOR DOSTOEVSKY   Peter Conradi
GEORGE ELIOT   Alan W. Bellringer
WILLIAM FAULKNER   David Dowling
GUSTAVE FLAUBERT   David Roe
E. M. FORSTER   Norman Page
ANDRÉ GIDE   David Walker
WILLIAM GOLDING   James Gindin
GRAHAM GREENE   Neil McEwan
ERNEST HEMINGWAY   Peter Messent
CHRISTOPHER ISHERWOOD   Stephen Wade
HENRY JAMES   Alan W. Bellringer
JAMES JOYCE   Richard Brown
D. H. LAWRENCE   G. M. Hyde
ROSAMOND LEHMANN   Judy Simons
DORIS LESSING   Ruth Whittaker
MALCOLM LOWRY   Tony Bareham
THOMAS MANN   Martin Travers
GABRIEL GARCÍA MÁRQUEZ   Michael Bell
VLADIMIR NABOKOV   David Rampton
V. S. NAIPAUL   Bruce King
GEORGE ORWELL   Valerie Meyers
ANTHONY POWELL   Neil McEwan
MARCEL PROUST   Philip Thody
BARBARA PYM   Michael Cotsell
JEAN-PAUL SARTRE   Philip Thody
SIX WOMEN NOVELISTS   Merryn Williams
MURIEL SPARK   Norman Page
JOHN UPDIKE   Judie Newman
EVELYN WAUGH   Jacqueline McDonnell
H. G. WELLS   Michael Draper
VIRGINIA WOOLF   Edward Bishop
PATRICK WHITE   Mark Williams

Forthcoming titles

MARGARET ATWOOD   Coral Ann Howells
IVY COMPTON-BURNETT   Janet Godden
JOSEPH CONRAD   Owen Knowles
JOHN FOWLES   James Acheson
FRANZ KAFKA   Ronald Speirs and Beatrice Sandberg
NORMAN MAILER   Michael Glenday
IRIS MURDOCH   Hilda Spear
PAUL SCOTT   G. K. Das
MARK TWAIN   Peter Messent

MACMILLAN MODERN NOVELISTS

GABRIEL GARCÍA MÁRQUEZ

Solitude and Solidarity

Michael Bell

First published 1993 by
THE MACMILLAN PRESS LTD
Houndmills, Basingstoke, Hampshire RG21 2XS
and London
Companies and representatives
throughout the world

ISBN 0-333-53765-3 hardcover
ISBN 0-333-53766-1 paperback

A catalogue record for this book is available
from the British Library

Printed in Hong Kong

Series Standing Order

If you would like to receive future titles in this series as they are
published, you can make use of our standing order facility. To place a
standing order please contact your bookseller, or, in case of difficulty,
write to us at the address below with your name and address and the
name of the series. Please state with which title you wish to begin your
standing order. (If you live outside the United Kingdom we may not
have the rights for your area, in which case we will forward your order
to the publisher concerned.)

Customer Services Department, Macmillan Distribution Ltd
Houndmills, Basingstoke, Hampshire, RG21 2XS, England.

Á la familia Rodriguez

'. . . closely related to conscientiousness is *loneliness* – it is perhaps only another name for it: that loneliness, you see, that is so difficult for the artist to differentiate from *public life.*'

'. . . that solidarity of conscience that binds an artist to his true public.'

Thomas Mann, *Reflections of an Unpolitical Man*

Contents

Acknowledgements

One of the pleasures of writing on García Márquez has been the intellectual hospitality of Latin American specialists. I wish particularly to thank John King, Edwin Williamson and Michael Wood for advice and encouragement. Also, as usual, Susan Bell.

A Note on Translation

All quotations from García Márquez' novels are given in Spanish followed by my own, fairly literal, translations but since most readers will be reading him in English I identify the translated passages with page references to commonly available English editions. Significant differences will be noted as they occur. Márquez' use of literary terms in ordinary contexts seems awkward in English and is often quietly dropped in translation. By the same token, the choice of words is clearly deliberate and often crucial to the larger meaning of the work in question.

General Editor's Preface

The death of the novel has often been announced, and part of the secret of its obstinate vitality must be its capacity for growth, adaptation, self-renewal and self-transformation: like some vigorous organism in a speeded-up Darwinian ecosystem, it adapts itself quickly to a changing world. War and revolution, economic crisis and social change, radically new ideologies such as Marxism and Freudianism, have made this century unprecedented in human history in the speed and extent of change, but the novel has shown an extraordinary capacity to find new forms and techniques and to accommodate new ideas and conceptions of human nature and human experience, and even to take up new positions on the nature of fiction itself.

In the generations immediately preceding and following 1914, the novel underwent a radical redefinition of its nature and possibilities. The present series of monographs is devoted to the novelists who created the modern novel and to those who, in their turn, either continued and extended, or reacted against and rejected, the traditions established during that period of intense exploration and experiment. It includes a number of those who lived and wrote in the nineteenth century but whose innovative contribution to the art of fiction makes it impossible to ignore them in any account of the origins of the modern novel; it also includes the so-called 'modernists' and those who in the mid- and late twentieth century have emerged as outstanding practitioners of this genre. The scope is, inevitably, international; not only, in the migratory and exile-haunted world of our century, do writers refuse to heed national frontiers – 'English' literature lays claim to Conrad the Pole, Henry James the American, and Joyce the Irishman – but geniuses such as Flaubert, Dostoevsky and Kafka have had an influence on the fiction of many nations.

Each volume in the series is intended to provide an introduction to the fiction of the writer concerned, both for those approaching him or her for the first time and for those who are already familiar with some parts of the achievement in question and now wish to place it in the context of the total *œuvre*. Although essential information relating to the writer's life and times is given, usually in an opening chapter, the approach is primarily critical and the emphasis is not upon 'background' or generalisations but upon close examination of important texts. Where an author is notably prolific, major texts have been made to convey, more summarily, a sense of the nature and quality of the author's work as a whole. Those who want to read further will find suggestions in the select bibliography included in each volume. Many novelists are, of course, not only novelists but also poets, essayists, biographers, dramatists, travel writers and so forth; many have practised shorter forms of fiction; and many have written letters or kept diaries that constitute a significant part of their literary output. A brief study cannot hope to deal with all these in detail, but where the shorter fiction and the non-fictional writings, public and private, have an important relationship to the novels, some space has been devoted to them.

NORMAN PAGE

1

Introduction

Given his world-wide popularity, it is not surprising that an enormous amount has been written on García Márquez. Much of the commentary is illuminating and I do not wish to repeat it except by way of necessary synthesis.[1] Nonetheless, the way in which I now wish to view his *œuvre* is partly by reconsidering this criticism and, through that, the nature and meaning of his popularity. For, as with Dickens, the deliberately popular note of the fiction has often successfully disguised its underlying complexity.

Much of the best commentary on Márquez came, naturally enough, in the wake of *One Hundred Years of Solitude* which was, and remains, his great popular and critical success. The understandable tendency at that point was to see this work as the imaginative goal to which his whole career had been striving. I believe this novel is, indeed, his most substantial work to date and that it is in many ways summative of the Marquesian themes. But in the light of the varied works produced over the two following decades, it emerges as increasingly untypical. It also lends itself to sentimentalised reading. One can, therefore, readily understand the attitude of grateful deprecation with which Márquez came to view it.[2] One can also understand the desire of critics to insist on its weight and complexity. But this is where the difficulty arises: what weight exactly should we give to its dark, if not pessimistic, historical vision; its mythopoeic allusions and structure; and, above all perhaps in terms of critical focus, to the pervasive and disarming humour which encompasses even the authority of the narrative form itself?

I wish to consider these questions, in the first instance, by placing *One Hundred Years of Solitude* within a close reading of Márquez' other fiction. In particular, I believe there is an implicit dialogue between his longer works. This internal dialogue does not necessarily resolve

1

the ambiguities and ambivalences which thoughtful readers have found in the individual works. It does something more important. It enables us to understand why these qualities are of the essence. Where a concentration on *Hundred Years* makes 'magical realism' into an artistic goal, my reading suggests this is itself only a particular vehicle for a more pervasive and fundamental concern for the nature of literary 'truth'.

Two principal schools of thought have grown up around *One Hundred Years of Solitude*. One stresses the fictive, mythopoeic and alchemical dimensions of the book and has therefore tended to universalise its significance.[3] The other readings, usually by regional specialists, emphasise the condensed accuracy of its historical vision which the former reading is likely to blur and sentimentalise.[4] In a general way it is evident that these readings are not incompatible and that the meaning of the book lies in their combination within the humorous spirit of the whole. But for a more precise sense of how this works it is well to be clear about such terms as 'myth', 'history' or 'realism' within the given imaginative context. The word 'myth' in particular has long acquired, whatever its anthropological and cultural implications, some specifically literary inflections. It can hardly be adduced as a fictive structure in the late twentieth century without a consciousness of its radical and programmatic significance for influential modernist writers such as James Joyce and Thomas Mann.

For this reason, I believe it is now most useful to see Márquez within a broader context of twentieth-century fiction around the world. His fiction was formed in immediate reaction to the Latin American writing of his early years but it also contributes to larger international developments. The distinctive imaginative modes, the political and historical themes, and the world-wide popularity of Márquez all make him a significant point from which to look back on previous generations which he, among others, enables us to see intelligibly *as* previous generations. The present study, therefore, has a comparative emphasis arising from the double sense in which it is necessary to 'locate' Márquez. Part of his meaning lies in his implicit place on a literary historical map of the century and part of it lies, in a deeply connected way, in his location on a map of the world.

In fact, the conflict, if it is one, between the universal and the local is a primary dialectic of Márquez' own writings. The critical conflict to date has been too often a symptomatic reflection, rather than an explication, of this dialectic. Márquez' *œuvre* is a sustained meditation on this very question: what is the relation between the local and the universal? These are clearly two aspects of a whole cloth. It is a kind of aspect blindness, as Wittgenstein put it, to see them as separable.[5] Nonetheless, as aspects, they are distinct and their difference can be important. Everything about Márquez' experience, including the sudden shift from an essentially local reputation to world popularity after the success of *One Hundred Years of Solitude*, encourages meditation on the ironies and involutions of this question. His twin themes of solitude and solidarity might even be seen as the extreme poles of this dialectic.

Márquez himself has identified the central theme of his work not as myth, or love, or politics, but solitude.[6] This is the continuing thread which links everything and I believe it remains the most helpful thread with which to enter his personal labyrinth; not least because solitude is itself a term of labyrinthine ambivalence. Solitude, for example, was central to the existentialist thinking of Sartre and Camus which had its ascendancy in France during Márquez' time in Paris. Márquez, like many Latin American writers, saw Paris as an effective cultural capital and he doubtless assimilated the existentialist emphasis on solitude as fundamental to the human condition. But Márquez always kept a critical distance from European culture and another, more immediately pertinent, discussion of solitude is Octavio Paz' volume of essays on Mexican history and character entitled *The Labyrinth of Solitude*.[7] In Paz, the starting point is a recognition of solitude as a peculiarly Mexican and Latin American experience; or rather perhaps that there is a peculiarly regional experience of solitude. And for Paz solitude was not simply negative. He saw it as a necessary part of human experience and as the traditional prelude to great action or creativity. In other words, within Márquez' formative horizon there was a strong awareness of universal, tragic solitude in modern literature at large along with a peculiarly local, and potentially creative, inflection of it.

It should also be noted that some of the characteristics Paz identified as Mexican and regional are ultimately part of the complex inheritance from Spain in Latin America. Like Paz, Márquez subjects this aspect of his own culture to a searching but inward critique. For both of them, solitude has a Hispanic as well as an American aspect.[8]

Paz argues that solitude may be experienced historically. The past, in other words, may seem to lack an intelligible or fruitful relation to the present. This too is a recurrent recognition in Spanish literature.

The Spanish writer 'Azorin' in 1905 followed the route of Don Quixote three hundred years after the original publication of Cervantes'
masterpiece.[9] Many later Latin American writers, including Márquez,
have looked consciously behind the European realist novel to find
a pertinent inspiration in the period, and in the specific figure, of
Cervantes. They too have followed the route of Don Quixote to find
him both remote and near. The example of Cervantes is not merely
'literary', it has an abiding historical pertinence.

As a modern Spaniard, 'Azorin' was struck, among other things, by
the similarity of the life, the landscape and the people of present-day
La Mancha to those described by Cervantes. At one level this was
rather charming, at another level it was shocking. It was as if life
had not moved on. And 'Azorin' develops this thought through
a mutual metaphor of history and landscape. As he looks on the
sun-baked, rocky terrain around him, there are no traces of human
impact between himself and the horizon, which is to say there are no
signs of historical activity within it.

> And we, having made our way for hour after hour across this
> plain, feel overcome, annihilated, by the unchanging flatness, by
> the transparent, infinite sky, and by the inaccessible distance. And
> now we understand how Alonso Quijano had to be born in this
> land, and how his spirit, unbound, free, had to take its frenetic
> flight through these regions of dream and illusion.[10]

Whether in time or in space, there is virtually no humanly significant
middle-ground. The eye passes from here to the horizon, or from
the present to the eternal, without a middle area of activity in which
their starkness can be absorbed.[11] *Don Quixote* is the story of a man
for whom eternal archetypes and the immediate present clash with
a disastrous absence of historical mediation. Cervantes' stroke of
genius was to find a fictional form in which to enact this theme.[12] The
achievement of several Latin American writers, including Márquez,
was to adapt his form to their own historical experience. Where Don
Quixote, the mad persona of Alonso Quijano, madly conflates the
chivalric past and contemporary life, several Latin American writers
have felt the weight of a past maddeningly compressed into their
present.

Because of his multilayered significance formally, historically and
philosophically, Cervantes remains a tutelary presence in this discussion of Márquez. But he is not the only point of reference. It is

necessary to see Márquez in a number of historical and comparative literary contexts simultaneously. For although he does not generally wear his metafictional concerns on his sleeve, his works are an intelligent digestion of, and an implicit commentary on, a variety of literary possibilities. Like Cervantes, he found himself at a historical and literary historical crossroads. As a further aspect of this, he is very self-consciously a local author with a world viewpoint, and while a regional readership will have a special insight into his work, the wider readership may ultimately be best placed to appreciate his significance. For example, 'magical realism' has acquired a strongly Latin American flavour but it is also a way of addressing fundamental questions about the nature of fiction.

What follows, therefore, is first a biographical summary concentrating on Márquez' formative years. The general questions broached in these introductory comments are then unfolded as they arise in his principal works. My brief is to discuss the novels and as it happens a concentration on the longer works rather than the stories helps to bring out the underlying shape and implicit dialectic of the *œuvre*. Part of the effect will be to highlight the peculiar position of *Hundred Years* within Márquez' *œuvre*; its being at once representative and untypical. Hence although the exigencies of exposition require me to lead up to and on from *Hundred Years*, the discussion may usefully be thought of as circling around this central text.

2

Biographical Summary

Gabriel Gárcia Márquez was born in 1928, the first child of a telegraph operator and the daughter of a retired colonel.[1] Partly in recompense for having married against their wishes, the couple allowed Gabriel, the first child, to be brought up by his maternal grandparents in Aracataca in the Caribbean coastal region of Colombia. Márquez has repeatedly affirmed the formative importance of both his grandparents who gave him not only love but also time, the latter often in the form of stories and reminiscences.

At the age of seven he left to go to school and to live with his parents who eventually settled in the capital, Bogotá, up in the Andean central region. He never liked this city, which represented the abrupt end of his childhood. When he revisited his childhood home with his mother in young manhood, the grandparents were dead and the town itself was in decline following the banana boom. The memory of this lost childhood, itself mixed up with a sense of region and history, was of crucial creative importance to him.

During his teenage years he formed the ambition to write and has spoken of Kafka's 'Metamorphosis' as the work which, in his student years, particularly brought home to him the power of imaginative literature. At university he studied law although he was distracted from the outset by writerly ambitions and soon started a career as a journalist. Between 1948 and 1949 he contributed many pieces to *El Universal* in Cartagena and then from 1950 to 1952, by now in his early twenties, he was living again in the Caribbean region, in the town of Barranquilla, and writing a regular whimsical column under the name of 'Septimus' for a local paper, *El Heraldo*.

His period in Barranquilla provided him with an important group of literary friends, including the older mentor figure Ramón Vinyes whom he was later to celebrate as the sage Catalan of *One Hundred*

Years of Solitude. He discovered modern writers, such as Virginia Woolf, who were to be significant models. The most important was William Faulkner whose narrative techniques, historical themes and small town provincial locations were a crucial example to several Latin American writers. His column would sometimes consist of a short fiction in the mode of Kafka or Hemingway. He also produced notes and extracts for a projected novel, then entitled *La Casa* (*The House*), about a family called Buendía.

In Barranquilla Márquez in effect provided himself with an excellent literary education on a world scale while also responding to the popular culture of the Caribbean world. From this point of view the inland capital, Bogotá, seemed relatively provincial and an ironic relation to its *capitolino* culture was one of the recurrent motifs of his column. But he subsequently moved to Bogotá and from early 1954 to mid-1955 he was a regular correspondent for *El Espectador*.

Here he took on two distinct functions both different from the humorous 'Septimus' persona. First, he was the regular film critic. This enabled him to develop his strong interest in film which remained important and became a primary and active concern again in the 1980s as he undertook teaching in the film school at Havana and became Head of the Latin American Film Foundation. His longer-term interest in film has a political dimension since it is a form which, in principle at least, could emulate the high periods of Greek and Elizabethan theatre when works of great power and subtlety reached the communal consciousness through large audiences, many of whom might be barely literate. His recent interest in television soap opera has a similar motive. The immediate importance of film to the early Márquez, however, was as part of a more general interest in narrative form and in the intelligent, artistic handling of popular material.

As well as film reviewing, Márquez now also took to investigative reporting. The 'Septimus' column had given him practice in developing a chosen theme economically, and usually with a need to hold the reader by the manner rather than the matter. Hence, as he turned to more factual, and often politically sensitive, subjects he brought to them a skilled consciousness of narrative presentation as in his account of an earthquake and avalanche at Medellin.[2] His most remarkable achievement in this respect was his series of columns telling the story in first person of a lone surviving sailor washed up after twelve days drifting at sea.[3] A Colombian destroyer had gone down as a result of its illegal overloading with domestic goods on a return journey from Houston. These articles were an effective exposure of the Colombian navy, and Márquez and the paper were put under some pressure not to publish.

Yet the story also lives on as his first extended narrative treatment of the themes of solitude and mortality as experienced within very specific political and historical conditions. The fact that the series was later published as a volume, *Story of Shipwrecked Sailor*, reflects its autonomous, or literary, interest.[4] Even when writing for a specific journalistic occasion Márquez was shaping it around permanent themes. Over this period he also completed *Leaf Storm* and the short story 'Tuesday Siesta', although the former was not published for some years.

In 1955 he was sent by his paper to Europe to report on a summit conference in Geneva. He remained in Paris, writing for *El Espectador* and then for *El Independiente*. When the latter in turn was closed down by the Colombian authorities, Márquez stayed on in poverty. Having himself experienced the non-arrival of subsistence cheques, he had written *No One Writes to the Colonel* by early 1957.

Márquez was thus in Europe during the suppression of the Hungarian revolution of 1956; an event which led to widespread resignations from the communist parties of Western Europe. Given his socialist convictions and his hostility to capitalist expansionism, particularly in the Third World, Márquez was reluctant to condemn the actions of the Russian-supported authorities in Hungary. This was to prove a distinctive, and for some a troublesome, aspect of his subsequent career that he would maintain relations with dictatorial figures, including Fidel Castro, rather than show unambiguous solidarity with liberal causes. The case of the Cuban poet, Hebertó Padilla, when Márquez refused to join a general protest against his treatment by the Castro regime, was a watershed moment in this respect.[5] This attitude has cost him friendships and has an important bearing on his fundamental sense of politics, and of human solidarity, as manifest in his fiction. Although he is clearly a deeply political man, his political thinking is evidently conducted in long-term historical and geo-political terms. More importantly, he wishes to place the political sphere itself within a larger sense of values. This is a running concern of his fiction which goes some way to vindicate, or explain, his outlook.

Towards the end of 1957 Márquez, by then in London, received an invitation from his friend Plinio Apuleyo Mendoza to help edit the weekly *Momento* in Caracas, Venezuela. From there, in 1958, he returned briefly to Colombia to marry Mercedes Barcha Pardo, whom he had known since their early teens. In May of that year, he and Mendoza resigned from the *Momento* over its apologetic editorial following popular demonstrations against the visit of the then US vice-president, Richard Nixon. Following the success of Fidel Castro's revolution, they both went to Cuba, where they saw the trial of one of Batista's generals, Sosa Blanco, which provided the original conception, albeit not then developed, for *Autumn of the Patriarch*.

Castro's regime set up a news organization, Prensa Latina, which was to make news available throughout Latin America despite the censorship of so many states in the region. Mendoza set up an office for Prensa Latina in Bogotá and invited Márquez to join him. Later, in 1959, the organisation sent him to Cuba and eventually to New York. When the position folded altogether in 1961, Márquez found himself again without resources but this time with a wife and child.

He went to Mexico to seek work in the film industry whereupon, as he recounts, he suddenly realised how to present the material of his long-standing project, '*La Casa*'. Approaching forty, he was able to draw on the unusually wide spectrum of writing experience he had acquired under the loose heading of journalism. He had also developed by the time of 'Big Mama's Funeral' an increasingly distinctive mode of fiction combining the condensed realism of Hemingway and Faulkner, as in 'Tuesday Siesta', with the radical fantasy of 'An Old Man with Enormous Wings'.[6] He was now able to write, in an eighteen-month burst, *One Hundred Years of Solitude*.

The critical and popular success of this book transformed his life and enabled him to produce in economic security a varied sequence of works including *The Autumn of the Patriarch* (1975), *Chronicle of a Death Foretold* (1981), *Love in the Time of Cholera* (1985) and *The General in his Labyrinth* (1989). For much of this time he lived partly in Mexico and partly in Barcelona. As a personal acquaintance of statesmen, and as a world-famous author, he has come to see power and fame from a new angle, including their disadvantages. His involvement in politics has remained active but has frequently been expressed through his personal relations with national leaders such as Fidel Castro, François Mitterrand and Daniel Ortega.

In recent years his interest in film has become active once more, partly for its own sake but more importantly as part of a renewed attempt to create the regional consciousness in Latin America which was the failed, or still to be achieved, ambition of Simón Bolívar. His interest still revolves around the same theme of solidarity outside of national political structures.

3

Journalism and Fiction

Fiction versus Politics?

In 1948, just at the outset of Márquez' career, the progressive political leader, Jorge Elizier Gaitan, was assassinated in Bogotá. The event sparked off popular disturbances which then spread from the capital and developed into a cycle of violence lasting for over a decade. There had been many similar periods of protracted violence in the history of Colombia. A number of writers addressed this theme in works known collectively as 'the novel of *La Violencia*'. Márquez devoted an article to this sub-genre in 1959, commenting on the low artistic quality of this overtly committed fiction which was performing something of the function of journalism.[1]

He goes on to argue that such journalistic purpose is intrinsically incompatible with artistic power. It is possible to recognise some *de facto* truth in this latter point without believing it is necessarily true in principle. It might be possible to combine both. The true interest of the article in the light of Márquez' own fiction over the same period is perhaps to show the strong resistance he himself found it necessary to make to the idea of a politically committed fiction even while producing a series of works which admirably answer to the double criterion. He clearly felt the need to write on political themes and his three first novellas, *Leaf Storm*, *In Evil Hour* and *No One Writes to the Colonel*, are all in some measure expressions of this motive. But they engage it as refracted through the Marquesian examination of character under stress and in conditions which are partly metaphysical. As with the story of the shipwrecked sailor, these fictions all encompass more permanent human themes.

More significantly, however, these novellas include a half-buried meditation on this very question of fiction and politics. It is often the case that creative writers do their most important and subtle thinking

11

in artistic rather than theoretical terms. If there is a disparity between Márquez' argument in the article and his fictional achievement in the 1950s this may reflect not so much a difference between theory and practice as differences in the quality of thinking to which, for a real artist, the two modes are susceptible. It is actually within his fiction that he 'thinks' most seriously, because concretely and inseparably, about this complex question. And the 'product' of the thinking remains irreducible to analytic terms. It is never an isolable idea, so much as a half-emergent consciousness within the works themselves.

i. The Outsider Within: *Leaf Storm*

Originally written as early as 1950–1, this first extended fiction of Márquez builds strongly on the example of Faulkner. It concerns the carrying out of a promise by a former colonel in the small town of Macondo to bury a man who, having claimed to be a doctor, has hanged himself in poverty and isolation after offending the townsfolk to the point where they wish him to rot unburied. The crucial moment of his rejection had come some years previously after his refusal to treat people wounded in a night of violent military suppression. The question of political violence hence lies at the root of the action without being its primary subject. The novella ends with the breaking open of the doctor's long-unused street door to take his body through the hostile town. Only in a later work of Márquez do we learn that the funeral passed off without challenge.

The story compresses the significant events of several decades by having its three narrators, the colonel, his daughter and her young son, recollect past events during their tense half hour by the doctor's body. The larger story is thus narrated not in the order of its chronology but as a gradual revelation of its inner logic. Furthermore, the three distinct life phases of the narrators give the narrative an increasing depth as of time strata. Starting with the innocent viewpoint of the young boy, the narrative passes to that of his thirty-year-old mother, and then in turn to that of the grandfather. As it finally returns to the 'voice' of the boy, we have a strong sense of return to the present with the past now inescapably locked within it. This past is not an inner, Faulknerian strain so much as an external situation of duty to a dead man, but the contrasting perceptions of the narrating characters, and the centrality of the corpse, point to a metaphysical theme about what it actually means to 'see', or know, other human beings.

The 'doctor', whose medical qualifications remain uncertain, had appeared mysteriously in the town as part of the general influx of drifters referred to in the title.[2] The arrival of a stranger is a frequent narrative catalyst in Márquez' fiction since his theme is often the incapacity to assimilate the outsider. In this first novella, the theme of the 'stranger' is central to the book and the doctor merely provides its principal focus. Much of the art of the narrative lies in the way the doctor's strangeness is made to pervade everything without being merely an external device. Márquez seeks to create a strangeness which is also perfectly natural. Some of his early attempts at fiction seek such an effect of strangeness but are merely, and pointlessly, weird.[3]

When the doctor's arrival is first announced to the Colonel's family by the servant, Meme, she says, and the narrative repeats the formulation,' . . . lo solicita un forastero . . . '[4] / ' . . . there's a stranger asking to see you . . . '.[5] The Spanish phrasing is more suggestive than the English. First, in the retrospect created by the context of flashback, the polite term 'solicita' takes on a sinister undertone of seduction. But more importantly the Spanish makes a significant discrimination within the general concept of the 'stranger'. The words 'forastero', 'fuereño' and 'fuerino' mean literally 'outsider'. By contrast, someone we merely happen not to know could be simply a 'desconocido' or 'unknown' to us. In other words, where this latter expression suggests a merely contingent condition the former terms suggest a more intrinsic one. The outsider may remain an outsider even when we get to know him. As used by Meme the word is innocent enough but within the overall narrative context it takes on the resonance of a mysteriously essential state. As with Camus' 'outsider', being a stranger proves to be this man's essential nature and function.[6]

Meme's introduction was the doctor's first appearance in the *life* of the colonel, but the *narrative* opens with his corpse. His suicide is his ultimate act of social withdrawal and Márquez, as he will throughout his work, treats death and solitude as mutual metaphors or as degrees of the same condition. Márquez exploits the continuity between the living and the dead which is to be found in much Caribbean and Latin American folk culture, such as the Mexican Day of the Dead, and, like the Mexican writer Juan Rulfo, he gives it a dark twist of his own.[7] Rather than a carnavalesque acceptance of death, we find the loneliness of death constantly anticipated in life and the loneliness of life echoed once again in death. The doctor's corpse is an epitome of, as much as a contrast to, his living state.

It is important to note that the doctor has made some awkwardly adolescent attempts to join the community before slipping into irremediable solitude and that his refusal to treat the town's wounded was not the beginning of their rejection of him. It is clear, in other words, that both sides are responsible. Or rather, perhaps, that a larger and less rationally comprehensible process has been taking place. At one point the colonel speaks of the doctor's 'laberíntica soledad' (p. 92) / 'labyrinthine solitude' (p. 65). If this is a direct allusion to Octavio Paz' title, it is appropriate. For Paz speaks of solitude as being a necessary and proper state at certain times, such as adolescence, and goes on to remark that such solitude would be a damaging symptom in maturity.[8] So too the doctor 'estaba viviendo una tardía y estéril adolescencia' (p. 79)/ 'was undergoing a belated and sterile adolescence' (p. 55). Yet although his mature regress into solitude is a sick condition, it has a further resonance precisely because he is not an adolescent. The colonel sees this condition with some pity and recognises it to be a more general possibility. As with Conrad's Lord Jim and Kurtz, the doctor's personal inadequacy reveals a universal potentiality which is commonly suppressed.[9]

Only the Colonel, and the former priest known as the Pup, seem aware of this; the Colonel more so than the priest. As we learn of the Colonel's contingent obligation to bury the dead man, we also become aware of a more essential relationship between them. Much as Conrad's Marlow finds with 'Lord' Jim and Kurtz, the initially contingent connection becomes the means to a general recognition occurring most crucially within the narrator himself. The Pup, who is the only other figure along with the Colonel to take effective responsibility in the community, likewise seems to see his own 'secret sharer' in the doctor with whom he has been doubled since their simultaneous arrival in the town.[10] On the one occasion he meets him he is unnerved. The townsfolk at large, on the other hand, simply reject the doctor. They have some cause, and that is part of the larger tragic conflict, but we also see their collective failure to recognise in themselves any echo of the abyss into which he has fallen. The town's failure to recover from the collapse of the banana boom, for example, is not ascribable simply to external and economic forces. It is another aspect of their projecting responsibility on to others.

The mutual isolation of the characters is embodied in the mode of the narrative itself. The compressed flashbacks present other characters essentially as they are remembered. As Proust knew very well, what exists in emotional memory exists as part of the remembering personality and often at a pre-conscious level. The past is necessarily a matter of imagination. When the daughter, Isabel, recollects her early acquaintance with her husband, Martin, who was soon to desert her, she says:

> ... y yo, sentada tres puestos más allá, veía al hombre que un año después sería el padre de mi hijo y a quien no me vinculaba ni siquiera una amistad superficial. (p. 89)

> ... and I, sitting three places away, looked at the man who a year later would be the father of my son and to whom I was not attached even by a superficial friendship. (p. 62)

The syntactical conflation of different times in this sentence was to become a central device of Márquez' fiction. A fundamental psychological structure is subliminally enshrined in the syntax. The original experience is no longer available to her separably from her awareness of their later relations. The superficial nature of the friendship was not so shocking at the time but Isabel invests the original situation with her later knowledge. At the same time, this later knowledge has not reduced, so much as confirmed, the superficiality of the acquaintance.

The compressed retrospect gives the relationship an ambiguous fatalism: it feels to her as if it were fated. It also makes Martin in some measure her imaginative construct. This latter effect is vital to the psychological action. In *The Rainbow* particularly, D. H. Lawrence used the image of the stranger, or 'foreigner', to enforce an intuition of the radical, and proper, otherness of all human beings.[11] Where that intuition of a radically different centre of life is lacking, other beings become merely opaque or, more commonly, they are unwittingly absorbed into our own emotional perception as we fail to see their separateness at all. Márquez uses the same image more bleakly to reinforce a sense of irremediable isolation and opacity. Even Conrad, by comparison, suggests a greater commonality of experience. His 'secret sharers', such as Kurtz and Lord Jim, are ultimately used to enforce an ethical solidarity in everyone.

This helps to explain why at certain times, such as Isabel's experience of marriage to Martin, characters feel a strong sense of *un*reality. If imagination is our way of understanding others, then it is as if her imagination can get no hold on him. And as she refuses merely to impose her own interpretation on him, whether maliciously or ideal-istically, she is effectively left with a blank in her reality. This contrasts with the townsfolk who make confidently collective interpretations. The people do not merely reject the doctor, they create an imagined figure by which to efface him and to justify their rejection. For them, his mystery is an empty space on to which they project a character.

The story of Isabel and Martin is indeed thematically vital although strictly irrelevant, from a literal point of view, to the main situation. This raises a general point about Márquez' handling of narrative. In his film criticism Márquez several times comments on the need for all the material to 'belong'. A given element may belong artis-tically without actually being a narrative necessity. He applauds the director Elia Kazan for so well integrating the priest figure in *On the Waterfront* (1954).[12] Although in Márquez' view the priest is not essential to the action, in watching the film we feel him to be. In Márquez' own case there is stronger point to be made: he frequently strengthens his thematic or narrative impact by deliber-ately importing extraneous material. Martin is such an element in *Leaf Storm*. Strictly, he has no bearing on the main action, or far less than the priest in *On the Waterfront*. But he reinforces the theme of the stranger in a different spirit from the doctor; superficially attractive but actually dangerous. He is thus a counterpoint to the doctor while also broadening this nuclear instance to encompass other relationships such as that of the colonel and his second wife.

The Martin story, in other words, acts as a deliberate distraction, thickening the narrative texture, so that the gradual revelation of the doctor's story takes on a parenthetic quality. Glimpsing one story through the other is both life-like and a means of artistic conden-sation. It is often hard, as indeed it should be, to say analytically how this works, how the one story affects the other, yet it seems crucial, particularly as compared with other early experiments in which Márquez sought to create a sense of mystery but leaned too directly on the 'mysterious' figure or event. The sense of mystery easily collapses into hokum. It is appropriate that the word 'mystery' once meant a 'craft' for there is an intimate relationship here between the substantive mystery of personality and the created mystery of narrative. In *Leaf Storm* Márquez has already learned to allow the really important effect to come to us unawares, wrapped up in something else. In his mature writing, this technique of indirection will come closer to the surface as a story-teller's game played more and more overtly with the reader.

In short, although the 'double' is a well-worn device of modern fiction, Márquez has already given it his own metaphysical inflection. It is part of a radical awareness in the narrative of the uncertainty of appearances. At a purely physical level, for example, the boy 'sees' his grandfather nearly knocked over by the mayor although the colonel has actually lost his balance momentarily in turning to face the mayor.[13] Even in this simple event there is clearly a deeper 'truth' in the boy's perception. And the whole narrative rests on radical and pervasive uncertainties: we do not strictly know whether the doctor was qualified; whether Isobel's husband Martin was truly a swindler; whether the townsfolk are indeed intending to interrupt the funeral and take revenge on the colonel's family; or even whether their attitudes are fairly represented by the colonel in the first place. These questions are not actively pursued, which might make them too self-conscious and technical. They are rather an appropriate penumbra of uncertainty; part of the opacity of solitude.

At the same time, these radical uncertainties mean that, within this story, the metaphysical theme of inescapable solitude, the recognition of 'the outsider within', stands almost in opposition to the political theme. There may be some contrastive force in the epigraph from Sophocles' *Antigone* over and above its obvious relevance to the narrative situation. In *Antigone*, all the parties understand the conflicting values, albeit with their different commitments. But the colonel acts with a patrician sense of duty in contrast to what he sees as the herdlike behaviour of the townsfolk. There is no mutual understanding. Yet although the possible viewpoint of the town's population remains unknown, we do know that they have suffered political violence and that this was the crucial occasion underlying their hostility to the doctor. Within the world of the narrative, therefore, the colonel's act of duty stands against a possible political solidarity which has herdlike overtones. There is some loading of the scales.

Even so, it is precisely by differing as to their values that the colonel and the townsfolk share the fundamental fact of interpretative uncertainty. Hence the Colonel sees them as making up 'malévolamente premeditado' (p. 81) / 'maliciously premeditated' (p. 57) gossip about the doctor and the barber's daughter although they seem convinced enough of their stories about him for the authorities to come and dig for Meme's body in the yard. At this point it is worth noting an affinity between such gossip and the creation of fiction; gossip being a version of the same underlying impulse. In this respect, some otherwise inconsequential details of the narrative suggest a subtextual preoccupation with the responsibilities of fiction.

The 'anonymous note' tacked to the doctor's door is a motif which will be expanded into the 'lampoons' of *In Evil Hour* where it pushes gossip towards a literal act of authorship. At the crucial moment when he refuses to tend their wounded the townsfolk shout ' . . . esa sentencia que aseguraría, para todos los siglos, el advenimiento de este miércoles' (p. 124) /' . . . that sentence which would make certain, for all time, the coming of this Wednesday' (p. 90). In Spanish, the word 'sentencia' has a primarily juridical sense which English assimilates to the grammatical meaning. As well as interpreting the doctor, they are now actively judging and determining his future. Malicious gossip is the sinister underside of the essential activity of ethical imagination by which we apprehend, and possibly help to create, others. That in turn is an act akin to fiction, which enables us, magically, to enter the fundamental solitude of another person. But Márquez most characteristically uses fiction not to perform this magical act of omniscience so much as to highlight its impossibility. The townsfolk seek to exert in reality a capacity that the narrative pointedly eschews even as a legitimate privilege of fiction.

Whether or not the townsfolk are purveyors of bad fiction, or usurpers of authorial privilege, these terms give a further edge to the interpretative uncertainties which have already been remarked within the work as a whole. For seen in this light the choice is not between fiction and 'reality' but between different qualities of imaginative projection, all arising from an irremediable isolation. In that connection it is suggestive that the colonel should see God as a lonely figure walking the night, while the atheistical doctor, of course, sees no one at all (p. 93 / p. 66). That the Creator himself might be a lonely outsider is indeed a theme to be developed later in the figure of Melquíades. In the immediate context the implication is that the colonel recognises solitude as a universal condition while the doctor, who epitomises the condition as suffered, has no such implicitly metaphysical insight into it. Where fiction is concerned, God is a traditional image of authorship and the reference to a solitary God, helpless or unwilling to affect the unfolding of events, suggests the necessary position of the author. The obligation of the author is more elusive than the colonel's. The author has to hold equally in creative understanding both the good and the evil characters. He can side with neither party and is bound by the inner logic of his creation.

These possible meanings are not actively thematised in this early work but a significant field of associations already lurks within the narrative. It is as if Márquez' imagination is constantly and subliminally recurring to the limits and dangers of the very faculty being exercised. His own use of imagination is disciplined by the polar images of damaging gossip and the absolute, yet ineffectual, responsibility of a lonely God. From the outset of his career, Márquez was drawn to modes of fable and fantasy. But, as with Cervantes and Flaubert, this impulse was countered by a strict respect for reality figured in literary terms as realism. The depiction of reality can never be, nor should it seek to be, merely passive or neutral. Yet imagination, the necessary instrument, is a two-edged sword. Even in this very early piece there is a sub-textual tension between these two necessary principles. Moments such as the boy's creative misperception of the colonel's fall are an anatomy of 'realism' in epitome. Maybe the success of Márquez' later mode, in which the fabular principle is so prominent, has been prepared for and is underwritten by the negative version of itself lurking implicitly in his *œuvre* even from this early work. The dark potential of the imagination continues to pervade Márquez' positive achievement as an ethical and artistic conscience.

This underlying tension can be felt stylistically in the story's careful combination of poetic resonance and apparently straight-forward descriptions of reality. This is not always successful, partly because of the first-person convention. The narrating characters have on occasion to use turns of phrase which seem beyond their likely range. For example, these thoughts attributed to Isabel:

> . . . y el reloj de le señora Rebeca cae en la cuenta de que ha estado confundido entre la parsimonia del niño y la impaciencia de la viuda, y entonces bosteza, ofuscado, se zambulle en la prodigiosa quietud del momento, y sale después chorreante de tiempo líquido, de tiempo exacto y rectificado, y se inclina hacia adelante y dice con ceremoniosa dignidad: 'Son las dos y cuarenta y siete minutos, exactamente'. (pp. 63–4)

> . . . and Señora Rebeca's clock comes to realize that it has been caught between the child's parsimony and the widow's impatience, and then it yawns, confused, plunges into the prodigious quiet of

the moment and emerges afterwards dripping with liquid time, with precise and rectified time, and leans forward to say with ceremonious dignity: 'It is exactly two forty-seven.' (p. 44)

Of course, a reader should not respond literalistically to realism which is only a literary convention like any other and many writers have successfully used the first-person method in a poetic way rather than as a means of characterisation. But even apart from a touch of over-writing here, every work establishes its own norms, and in *Leaf Storm* the reality effect which is vital to the narrative depends in significant measure on this convention being taken seriously. At such moments, therefore, we do notice the 'poetic' as overlaid on the realism. But such moments hardly impair the effect of the whole. Indeed, one would rather say that whenever it seems to have been a choice Márquez has rightly gone for the more resonant language. The final moment when the doctor's door is broken down and the light floods into the room is a magnificently 'simple' compression of the story's pent-up emotions into an apparently physical description. This is only possible because of a pervasive heightening of perception throughout.

Márquez was to acquire a greater skill in managing the levels of his narrative language and his next extended works are not in the first person. But in the longer term it is important to note that there should have been from the outset a tension, as well as mutual assimilation, of the 'poetic' and the 'realistic'. Ultimately he wishes not just to elide the distinction but to exploit it. The stylistic tension in this early tale is a creative growing point through which he will continue to meditate on the Cervantean theme of the vital but ambivalent power of imagination.

ii. 'Saving the Appearances': *No One Writes to the Colonel*

Márquez' next published novella was written in Paris after he had himself experienced the situation of awaiting, without other resources than the charity of friends, possible subsistence cheques. The story concerns an elderly colonel and his wife in a small Colombian town who are still awaiting, after fifteen years, the military pension due to him for his service in the civil war. Their son, Augustín, has been killed nine months previously for distributing clandestine news-sheets despite political censorship and the couple are left only with his fighting cock which has become the focus of parental and political feeling. Although they are both desperate with hunger, and the wife is in serious ill-health, the colonel refuses to sell the cock or to give up hoping for the arrival of his pension. Since Márquez' briefer taste of a similar situation had been caused by the Colombian regime's closing of his paper, it is not surprising that the political dimension of this story is more evident than in *Leaf Storm*, yet it is still refracted through a lens of imaginative concentration around a metaphysical theme.

The story has a concentrated simplicity which is evidently modelled in part on the early Hemingway. Dispensing now with first-person narrative, its technique is to see intently through the colonel's eyes without necessarily seeing into him. At one point the colonel talks to the doctor while watching the arrival of the week's post. As the doctor is speaking we are told:

> Pero el coronel estaba pendiente del administrador. Lo vio consumir un refresco de espuma rosada sosteniendo el vaso con la mano izquierda. Sostenía con la derecha el saco del correo.[14]

> But the colonel was hanging on the postmaster. He saw him consume a drink of pink froth holding the glass in his left hand. In his right he held the postbag.[15]

The short factual sentences insist on our seeing only what is physically perceived yet the colonel's *non*-attention to the doctor at this moment creates an unspoken intensity which the reader shares. Although the technique is essentially simple, it is used with a skill that makes the simplicity deceptive. To unpack this a little without losing the simplicity of effect it is helpful to think of it as 'filmic', for in prose narrative a filmic effect is never literally so; it is necessarily a studied technique.

Márquez himself was quite conscious that this work, even more than his other early pieces, was the fruit of his many years of thinking about film. Márquez' review, only a year or so earlier, of de Sica and Zavattini's *Umberto D* (1952) catches several relevant aspects of his own art. The film followed with minute closeness the everyday actions of an ordinary, solitary and almost anonymous individual. Márquez comments:

> A story equal to life must be told by the very method that life itself uses: giving to every minute, to every second, the importance of a

decisive event. De Sica and Zavattini have divided the action into infinitesimally small spaces and affirmed the tremendous pathos that lies in the simple act of going to bed, of returning home; in the simple, inevitable and transcendental fact of existing for a second.[16]

The opening declaration here is a ringing affirmation of artistic principle although it does not yield much in the way of analytic sense. Indeed, Márquez' own subsequent analysis of the film suggests that life does not usually appreciate itself in this way; hence the value of the film and the need to explain its value.

The rhetorical generality of the statement points rather to Márquez' constant underlying meditation on the double truth that life is appreciated through art, and therefore through a technique of presentation, and yet technique must always be an emergent function of the life in question. Whenever the technique of a work of art is actually worth talking about you are already talking about something more than technique. This remains an important recognition for Márquez although by the same logic it will not for the most part be a too explicit theme within his work. In becoming explicit it would be likely to become emptily external. Márquez' artistic commentary, on film or literature, tends to be intelligently pregnant without being closely analytic or technical. His analytic intelligence goes where it really matters, into the technique of creation where it similarly disappears into the subject.

As Márquez goes on to describe the specific achievement of the film, several points of similarity to *No One Writes* become evident. It is said of the colonel too: 'Hacía cada cosa como si fuera un acto trascendental' (p. 54) / 'He did everything as if it were a transcendental act' (p. 6). The slow concentration on ordinary actions suggests they have an importance somehow beyond themselves yet purely immanent. In this respect, the word 'transcendental' is precise enough for its purpose as used both in the review and in the novella yet its precision includes a measure of deliberate indeterminacy. What exactly is the significance that is being seen in common actions? In the film review this is attributed to a metaphysical recognition: the usually unnoticed wonder of conscious existence. In the colonel's life it clearly has a different emphasis: his determined, quixotic resistance to the crushing pressure of poverty, uncertainty and political injustice. In both contexts, however, the two aspects are inseparable and hence the appropriateness of using a single word to cover both. De Sica's film, for example, whatever the truth of Márquez' comments, also reflects the specific historical conditions of life in post-war Italy. The metaphysical appreciation of common experience is likely to arise from some immediate pressure while the local pressure often takes its interest from the metaphysical recognition to which it gives rise.

Beckett, for example, uses a related art of reductive compression in a clearly metaphysical spirit. Kafka uses his in a puzzling middle area which deliberately lends itself to political, religious, psychological and metaphysical readings. Márquez is at the other end of the spectrum from Beckett in giving a specifically political context, but the cousinship is as important as the difference. The colonel's experience produces a meditation on the nature and value of life akin to these more overtly metaphysical writers. This is not an alternative, or somehow extra, to a political reading. The colonel's dignity as a conscious individual being is the standard by which political evil is to be judged. To that extent, it is in itself a form of political resistance. But more importantly, the 'metaphysical' can never be separated from the 'political' and Márquez' characteristic territory is their interaction. Márquez' implicit meditation on the value of conscious life underwrites the colonel's homely form of political assertion.

That may partly explain a measure of ambiguity about the figure of the colonel which the 'filmic' technique, as suggested by the comments on *Humberto D*, helps to create. For the technique gives a great sense of intimacy without actually needing to take us into the colonel's consciousness. This is crucial since the colonel requires a certain simplicity of character into which it might be damaging to enquire too closely. One of the dangers of the subject is sentimentality; including the apparently anti-sentimental toughness to which Hemingway was susceptible. Márquez loathes cheap emotional appeal, but this is because he appreciates genuinely simple and popular feeling. He does not fear, or need strenuously to avoid, sentimentality.

The artistic, or psychological, problem at the heart of this story is that the colonel must remain a figure of serious, and unsentimental, interest. This fundamental premise would be threatened if he seemed merely stupid yet his whole posture depends on something dangerously akin to stupidity. As his wife says, he needs the 'paciencia de buey' (p. 82) /'patience of an ox' (p. 22) to go on waiting for fifteen years. The image deflects attention from bovine stupidity to endurance but it does so by incorporating it; by recognising it as the necessary condition of his heroic obstinacy.

So too, Márquez presents the colonel as childlike. Apart from being constantly put in the position of a child, the colonel seems also to have the positive innocence of one. This in itself could be sentimental if it were the only note in his character but in his case it rather prevents his male toughness from being too merely that. He is of a generation which left school to go to fight in the civil war and even now his attempt to pen a letter is like that of a school child.

> Escribió con una compostura aplicada, puesta la mano con la pluma en la hoja de papel secante, recta la columna vertebral para favorecer la respiración, como le enseñaron en la escuela. (p. 91)

> He wrote with a studied composure, his writing hand resting on the blotting paper, his spine straight to aid his breathing, as he had been taught at school. (p. 27)

His straight back combines the military and the childlike. He seems to be approaching his second childhood without having really left the first, as if he has been robbed of the life in between. This is not merely the pathos of a victim. On the contrary, the colonel has a positive naïvety on which the whole action rests.

Márquez' success is to create a sense of intimacy with the colonel while preserving an ambiguity as to his precise consciousness. This is achieved partly by physical intimacy, including the most private functions and sensations of the body, which gives him a concrete dramatic presence and disguises the essential lack of access to his mind. Time and again, his emotional experience seems to be felt directly as bodily sensation. At the same time, this communicates, in a dramatic and implicit way, the extent to which he himself apparently does not have much access to an inner life either. Indeed, we understand him to be someone who survives partly by not enquiring too closely into himself but rather by living up to a code; even when that code seems to have little purchase on the world. It is no wonder that his body should respond so vividly to what his consciousness largely denies. His body absorbs, and expresses, his anxieties.

His wife is also important in this connection. Most obviously, she is a foil expressing the pressures to which he refuses to succumb or the attitudes he refuses to adopt. For example, whereas he identifies the fighting cock with Augustín's life, and makes sacrifices accordingly, she associates it with his death and would prefer to be rid of it. The wife can also be seen, a little more intimately, as an *alter ego* representing what the colonel has to repress in himself. Yet it is not, for all that, a psychological study of unconscious processes. One might rather say that the colonel is a pre-Freudian being and the narrative method consciously respects him for what he is. Between his inner code and the external chaos he *allows* no introspective middle ground. Just before the taut thread of his commitment to his code finally snaps he sees an image of himself in the fighting cocks: 'Le pareció una farsa a la cual – voluntaria y conscientemente – se prestaban también los gallos' (p. 140) / 'It seemed to him a farce to which – in a quite voluntary and conscious way – the cocks were also lending themselves' (p. 55). His imagining the cocks as endowed with consciousness is the mirror image of his own studious avoidance of consciousness. In other words, as a conscious being he aspires to their unconscious being. He deliberately deflects his consciousness on to his perceived duty rather than inwards on to himself or outwards on the full reality of the world. He also 'knows' he is lending himself to a farce but he won't allow that recognition any more intimate mental hospitality than its indirect reflection in the birds.

For such an anachronistic character an antique method of narrative is appropriate. Most commentators have noted the quixotic nature of the colonel but the force of the allusion, and its narrative implications, are worth pausing on. The elusiveness of the colonel's consciousness, combined with his insistence on living up to code embodied in appearances, is reminiscent of *Don Quixote*, whose consciousness is similarly veiled from the reader and even, to some ambiguous extent, from himself. We don't know exactly how intelligent the colonel is any more than we know how mad is Cervantes' hero. At one level, the ruses by which the old couple disguise their poverty, such as the wife's boiling stones at meal-times or the colonel's patched shirts being hidden under his coat, are an echo of the poverty-stricken knight in *Lazarillo de Tormes* (1554) who goes out to walk at dinner time so as not to admit his hunger and poverty even to his servant, Lazarillo. That knight was presented satirically and was a precursor of Don Quixote whose mental derangement arose in part from his idleness, from the lack of any real function for the social class he represents. Lazarillo's master was keeping up appearances in a purely social sense and in Márquez' story this attitude corresponds

to that of the colonel's wife. The colonel, by contrast, is more like
Don Quixote, whose madness had a metaphysical edge and a partial
self-consciousness reflecting a larger shift in world view occurring
in Cervantes' time. Owen Barfield has explained this shift as a
loss of meaning in the traditional philosophical phrase 'saving the
appearances'.[17]

Barfield remarks that, to a modern ear, this phrase suggests merely
some kind of genteel hypocrisy. But up till the time of Kepler and
Galileo (and, we might add, Cervantes) it had a serious implication
of something like 'accounting for the phenomena'. That is to say,
the activity of astronomers had been to provide the most simple and
reliable ways of describing the movements of the heavenly bodies.
How exactly they moved was God's affair. It had been recognised
since classical times that it was possible to calculate these movements
by taking the sun rather than the earth as the fixed point and with
Copernicus this came to be the preferable method. Hence, Barfield
explains, the shock of Galileo's heliocentric hypothesis was not so
much that it was heliocentric but that it was a new theory about the
very nature of reality. If it is so much easier to describe the heavens
'as if' the earth were going round the sun, then the earth must be
doing so in fact.

There is a close parallel here with Don Quixote, who did not just
mistake the appearance of windmills for giants or flocks of sheep for
armies. He went on believing in his account of the phenomena long
after the appearances had become unambiguous even for him. He
constantly 'saved the appearances' by hypothesising an enchanter,
an anticipation of Descartes's evil demon, who made the armies,
for example, appear to be sheep. For a typically modern consciousness, as science replaced religious faith, the pre-Galilean attitude
to astronomy came to seem almost as absurd, and as evidently
self-deceiving, as Quixote's carefully protected illusions. Modern
realist fiction was born of this philosophical shift.

The colonel's obstinate commitment to his own values shares,
at a more humble level, something of this deliberate refusal to
accept either the logic of appearances or the inappropriateness of
his code. He takes it upon himself to maintain an order of values
in despite of appearances and without either the alibi of madness
or the comfort of a shared belief. Whereas Cervantes and his hero
were still Christian, the colonel is obliged, in a post-religious world,
to go it alone. He affirms values of justice and honour which have no
metaphysical or social support. As in Cervantes, these significances

are communicated to us as readers without our being sure how much they are appreciated in this way by the character. The uncertainty gives it the sense of psychological depth. The colonel is not merely a lay figure representing an abstract principle.

Barfield's remarks also suggest that the ultimate justification of such Quixotry is religious, although in the colonel's case religious terms can only be invoked obliquely. Hence *No One Writes* has a number of religious allusions which, beyond their locally satiric effect, obliquely underwrite the colonel's code. While the colonel is writing his letter to the authorities setting out his case, his wife recites the rosary. She tells him the date of his inclusion on the pension list without interrupting herself (p. 27 / pp. 91–2). This suggests both the externality of her ritualised prayer and its essential parallel to his pursuit of the pension. It too is a kind of ritual affirming a spiritual reality that cannot be proven. Hence the externality is not simply satirical; it has a serious point. Traditional Catholic ritual was knowingly external because it was properly concerned with a disposition of the will rather than the feelings. In confession, the penitent is obliged to *be* sorry rather than wait till *feeling* sorry since feelings are not necessarily to be commanded nor are they always a reliable index of ethical significance. In other words, the affirmation of a spiritual value may have, on occasion, to be irrespective of the state of personal feeling and will be expressed in a formal observance or, in other words, at the level of appearances.

When, therefore, the priest declares that the old couple cannot sell their wedding ring because it is a sin to trade in sacred objects, we are not impressed by his humanity or his spiritual insight but we are in a better position to understand the importance to the colonel of not selling the game-cock. The cock has for him an absolute value such that selling it would be comparable to the sin of simony. Simony may be a relative moral failing but it rests on the absoluteness of a taboo. The colonel's code has the expressive significance of a religious observance set against both worldly values and personal feeling. He is in the proper sense a martyr, or witness, for a value which he perhaps knows to lie beyond the phenomenal appearances of his world.

In sum, the externally 'filmic' method of the narrative is deeply appropriate to the character and significance of the colonel, including his aura of deliberate archaism. The technique makes his relative lack of psychological inwardness both compelling and natural. But, as has been said, the term 'filmic' is strictly a metaphorical description of a narrative effect. Language is never literally filmic and indeed the very closeness with which the effect of film is imitated rather highlights the literary nature of the medium in which this is being done. At the local stylistic level, we may say that, whereas *Leaf Storm* showed some occasional strain between the literal demands of its narrative convention and the poetic aspirations of the narration itself, this next story is more spare in its language while allowing a poetic resonance to develop over the heads of the characters. This is commonly a matter of introducing what seem at first to be innocently literal details which are then echoed with a progressive depth of association, such as the increasingly funereal umbrellas, the religious allusions just mentioned, and of course the central motif of the fighting cock.

But there is also a more structural dimension to the story's poetic concentration. Once again, it is an artistic deftness which does not damage its apparent simplicity. I have suggested some reasons why the colonel's precise perception of his circumstances should be handled largely by inference. He is not an introspective man. The artistic need for this indirection is increased by an implicit double time in the story; a technique most famously used by Shakespeare, in, for example, *Hamlet* and *Othello*, where he packs into a poetic drama an experience that strictly requires the extended time-scale of a novel.[18]

Whereas *Leaf Storm* had a series of flashbacks this story packs its past, and the political conditions, more casually and indirectly into its present narrative. We follow the colonel through a series of actions culminating in the last word when he finally breaks his own code of decorum, and specifically linguistic decorum, which has been established throughout the work. This means that, as readers, we are going through the colonel's experiences with the freshness of narrative novelty while understanding that for him they are all part of a long-repeated ritual. We are constantly assured that his hopes and disappointments retain the intensity of a first occasion such as they are to us. On the whole this is dramatically effective although there are moments when it is difficult to dwell on the implied deep time of memory and repetition without questioning the credibility of the colonel's present response. In conversation with his lawyer, for example, when given the cliché comfort that

La unión hace la fuerza.
En este caso no la hizo – dijo el coronel, por primera vez dándose

cuenta de su soledad – . (pp. 84–5)

'Unity is strength'
'Not in this case,' said the colonel, becoming aware for the first
time of his solitude – . (p. 24)

The last clause is hard to credit if we pause to reflect on the span
of time implied. It depends on our remaining within the dramatic
impact of the narrative present. Or a few pages earlier we are told
'sintió el terror' (p. 81) / 'he was terrified' (p. 21) when the doctor
asks the postmaster whether there are any letters for the colonel. And
this is a particularly crucial moment since it leads the postmaster to
utter the title sentence of the whole tale.

At such moments the real point is our narrative experience rather
than the experience attributed to the colonel. It is unlikely, in other
words, that one could really contemplate these responses of the colonel as psychologically probable after so many years of repetition. An
attempt to do so would raise the spectre of the colonel as personally
obtuse rather than heroically persistent. But Márquez' skill lies in
making us feel the weight of this past without engaging too inwardly
with the point where the two times have to meet: in the mind of the
colonel. If there are moments when, on closer inspection, we can see
the joins in the fabric of the narrative, these moments confirm the
general success and perhaps even act as a hint that the story does not
ultimately ask to be read in a purely naturalistic spirit.

In sum, the narrative is formally naturalistic and depends on this
to communicate the claustrophobic atmosphere of the colonel's, and
the general political, situation. Yet closely considered, this naturalism
is, as it usually is, an artistic sleight of hand. The real interest of
the colonel is 'transcendental'. He has gone into the army as an
adolescent and we encounter him now as the helpless 'orphan' of his
own son. Márquez' artistic tact makes it crass to ask too closely about
the years of his maturity. We implicitly understand that the colonel is
the summative symbol for a deeply representative experience of life.
He is a means of condensing, rather than laboriously rehearsing, this
experience. The story leads us to leap to this level of concentrated
significance while gathering into itself the social and historical foreground of the overtly naturalistic form.

Once again, even in his most naturalistic mode, Márquez has an
artistic cunning and concentration which essentially escape, even
while encompassing, the terms of naturalism. At the opening of the

last section, the colonel looks out on his 'marvellous' / 'maravilloso' patio in the morning air to see 'la hierba y los árboles y el cuartito del excusado flotando en la claridad, a un milímetro sobre el nivel del suelo' (p. 135)/ 'the grass and the trees and the cubicle of the privy floating in the clear air, one millimetre above the ground' (p. 52). In truth, the whole story is one millimetre off the ground. The feat is not noticeable to the naked eye yet strictly defies the laws of reality.

The preceding discussion may help to explain Márquez' own ambivalent response to this novella. Speaking later in his career, he saw it as his most successful achievement before *Chronicle of a Death Foretold*.[19] Yet he has also included it, along with the other novellas of an overtly political kind preceding *One Hundred Years of Solitude*, as relatively narrow in its focus and effect.[20] It seems to me that it is indeed an artistic triumph because of the way it recognises and exploits the limits of its material. As with Jane Austen, the limits are a means of artistic concentration. Moreover, it is a triumph for which the careful lack of psychological inwardness is crucial. The colonel is the vehicle for a concentrated vision, and an affirmation of value, which depend on his isolation from us as well as from other characters. The story makes us see through the eyes of solitude.

iii.   'Bursting to Talk': *In Evil Hour*

In the course of Márquez' first three novellas, at least in their order of publication, the political theme becomes progressively more overt and central although he continues to handle it with a concentration on permanent human questions which both transcend and enrich the political material. The doubleness is all. Hence if one reads the early Márquez, with the hindsight of *Hundred Years*, as moving towards 'magical realism', then *In Evil Hour* seems quite evidently a step in that direction. But if one sees him as constantly negotiating a fundamental tension between different imperatives then *No One Writes* and *In Evil Hour* rather represent two different imaginative possibilities within the same general debate. Either could be seen as a step 'forward' depending on your viewpoint.

Overall, *No One Writes* is perhaps superior with its intense, flickering concentration on the figure of the colonel. *In Evil Hour* is comparatively diffuse but it offers a different kind of interest in relation to the present theme of fiction and politics. Indeed, it is remarkable that just as *In Evil Hour* presents its political subject-matter more directly so at the same time, as if by a compensatory necessity, its fictional medium is also raised to a new point of self-consciousness. Once again, however, this remains still very implicit and the implicitness is an important part of the meaning. Fictional self-consciousness never becomes an abstract or essayistic issue separable from the action.

In Evil Hour describes the return to brutal political repression in a small town which has enjoyed a respite during a change of policy by the national regime. The return to previous conditions is largely sparked by anonymous notices, or lampoons, posted around the town with gossip about the private lives of individual citizens. These lampoons are essentially unpolitical in their personal subject-matter yet they seem to arise from, and to have an impact on, the political conditions. As a form of gossip they also have an implication for the nature of the fiction in which they appear. For gossip is not only allied to fiction, in the present case it becomes a way of significantly defining the world of the fiction.

The authorship of the lampoons remains a mystery. We don't know if they are the work of an individual or, as is suggested at one point, of the whole town. In an important sense, of course, they are the work of the town. They express the condition of the community. But the mystery also raises a question about the nature of the fiction we are reading. On the one hand, the device of the lampoons can be accepted naturalistically. We simply don't know who is responsible for them. Or else it pushes the naturalistic narrative to a symbolic edge reminiscent of Muriel Spark's *Memento Mori* (1959) in which a number of elderly characters receive mysterious phone calls reminding them that they must die. As with the lampoons, this message in itself is not news but putting it into words is disturbing to most of the recipients. And similarly, as with the lampoons in *In Evil Hour*, the characters' responses are indicative of their different ethical natures. In Spark's Catholic novel, it becomes evident that we are to understand the calls as having a supernatural origin as she wittily plays with naturalistic expectations generally and with the rationalist conventions of detective fiction in particular. She is playing a fictional game for a metaphysical purpose. The *memento mori* is directed at us rather than the characters. In comparison, Márquez stays just within naturalistic terms but he nonetheless uses the lampoons to generate a comparably disturbing psychological and symbolic force. We are never quite sure how to take them: whether as a psychological manifestation of communal conditions or as a fictional *deus ex machina*. The latter points to a meta-fictional adumbration of the novel's naturalistic theme. This story seems to be more than just one millimetre off the ground but the interest of this is not the possible move towards 'magical realism' so much as a concern for the meaningfulness of fiction at large.

To appreciate this it is first necessary to note what the naturalistic themes are. Solitude remains a central question in this story but the emphasis of *Leaf Storm* and *No One Writes* is reversed: instead of focusing on the isolation of one individual, it studies a collective experience of mutual solitude. The repeated expression 'Ustedes', rendered in the standard English translation as 'You people', expresses the felt divisions in the community from which the individual isolation stems. From the patrician standpoint of the colonel in *Leaf Storm*, it was necessary to distinguish mob collectivity from genuine community and it is initially tempting to say of the small town in *In Evil Hour* that it has no real community. But that is perhaps to miss the point. The story rather affirms the ineradicable instinct to community through the distorted form in which this need gets expressed under the adverse conditions imposed by the regime.

This change of emphasis goes with a shift from Faulknerian compression of the individual past to a social interaction in the present for which Virginia Woolf provides the more appropriate model. Márquez once remarked that he would have been a different writer if he had not read at the age of twenty a sentence from *Mrs Dalloway*.[21] His naming one of his characters Mr Carmichael suggests a parenthetical compliment to Woolf.[22] The sentence in question, a description of an official car, is worth quoting both for its general relevance to Márquez and for the way he transforms the Woolf mode in this story.

> But there could be no doubt that greatness was seated within; greatness was passing, hidden, down Bond Street, removed only by a hand's-breadth from ordinary people who might now, for the first time and last, be within speaking distance of the majesty of England, of the enduring symbol of the state which will be known to curious antiquaries, sifting the ruins of time, when London is a grassgrown path and all those hurrying along the pavement this Wednesday morning are but bones with a few golden wedding rings mixed up in their dust and the gold stoppings of innumerable decayed teeth.[23]

Márquez was struck by Woolf's invocation of a vast and destructive vista of time which was the germ of *One Hundred Years of Solitude*. Her phrase 'will be known' anticipates the fateful 'había de'/'was to' formula which is a stylistic trademark of that book. And Márquez, like Woolf, is remarkable for the number of his works in which the very titles allude to time. So too, her concentration on the emptiness, yet reality, of power as invested in the car rather than the unknown occupant was a hint, Márquez says, for *The Autumn of the Patriarch*. Above all, we may suppose him to have been attracted by the elusive tone of the passage. Its obvious seriousness is protected by an incipient self-parody, a conscious rhetorical extravagance, which 'was to' prove equally important to Márquez.

But the immediate point of the comparison in relation to *In Evil Hour* is to see how Márquez has assimilated Woolf's techniques to his own expressive needs. In effect, he has reversed their impact. A common reservation about Woolf has always been that dependence on the heightened sensibility of her usually upper middle-class characters ultimately yields a too-glancing relation to the historical world in the novels. This can be felt in the present passage. Taking *Mrs Dalloway* at large, Woolf invokes a sense of twentieth-century history through Septimus Smith, a psychologically damaged survivor of the Great War, and by other allusions such as Clarissa Dalloway's politician husband. Yet the narrative mode of the novel draws all these large topics into the inner world of the heroine, Clarissa. At the climactic scene of her party, the social medium exists primarily in her consciousness. It was, of course, part of Woolf's modernist achievement to do this, but a question inevitably hangs over this achievement.

In Márquez, by contrast, the outer world has an overwhelming reality. For him, the conjunction of personal emptiness and effective power in the official car would be likely to be felt as an oppressive, if paradoxical, weight whereas Virginia Woolf has an ambivalent, incipiently sentimental, acquiescence in the mystification. Her method depends on, or at least encourages, this. So too, when the chimes of Big Ben sound through *Mrs Dalloway* their poetic resonance, and their modernist spatialising of the narrative are a little self-conscious as a device, but the curfew which sounds in *In Evil Hour* gives the same technique a natural and chilling force. Whereas in *Mrs Dalloway* it is only Clarissa's and Woolf's heightened sensibilities which feel the weight of mortality in the ordinary sound of the bell, in Márquez an oppressive military signal has been naturalised, by sheer habit, into a mere time-piece. If Woolf's characters seek to expand consciousness, Márquez' want rather to deaden it. Time in the story is constantly experienced as a bodily sensation. The return of air-raid sirens and gun-shots, for those unfortunate enough to have a personal experience of them, will commonly act in the first instance through what Proust called the affective memory. The memory is likely to be first felt as a rising panic in the guts.

Márquez, then, has adapted the technique of Woolf to an opposite significance. Where she typically absorbs the world into a heightened consciousness, he expresses the absorption of personal consciousness into the physical and social worlds. Hence, for a different reason from in *No One Writes*, there is a similar refusal to dwell in the consciousness of the major characters. In fact the central creative problem of *In Evil Hour* is the absence of an arena of personal consciousness in which to explore the theme of political evil.

For Márquez is facing as a creative problem what Hannah Arendt, when she attempted to comment on the Eichmann trial, faced journalistically as the 'banality of evil'.[24] What Arendt found most truly shocking about the typical perpetrators of mass evil in this century was their personal vacuity. Their purely instrumental emptiness affords no insight into the nature of the evil they have performed. Tyranny not only enters the tissues of everyday life, it gets to be treated as if it were itself an everyday fact. Evil often arises from a moral blankness which it in turn exacerbates. Lieutenant Calley's comment on the My-Lai massacre in Vietnam was evidently, and numbingly, sincere: 'It was no big deal, Sir.'[25]

Márquez engages this problem directly in the corrupt mayor and police chief. He opens the whole story strategically by giving the mayor the common human vicissitude of a toothache. Márquez thus prevents the mayor being separated off as simply a monster. And some of the mayor's later actions seem to have, at first, a crudely public-spirited intention. When he tells the homeless people to settle on town land, we do not yet know that he will turn this to his own financial advantage. And to an extent this impression remains. We understand that, although he is consistently on the make, the evil that he does is partly reactive. Hence, when it comes to the horrific castration and killing of a young man in police custody the well-established moral vacuity of the mayor is part of the horror. Having no integral self he acts according to his surroundings and even in the final descent into brutal suppression we sense his grotesque conviction of public duty.

Márquez' problem is to present this banality without himself being banal. Of course, he could have concentrated on the cruelty from the victim's point of view and left the perpetrator as a monster. Such fiction has an important function but it is as if Márquez sees the temptation of a one-sided response as being one to resist, and to make the reader resist. For the mayor's corruption is as enigmatic as was the colonel's tenacity in *No One Writes*. Both characters resist being a Jamesian arena of consciousness. In this situation, the anonymous lampoons are Márquez' strategic means of by-passing personal consciousness. What cannot be dealt with directly may be handled indirectly.

Márquez enunciates the general principle in the review of *Umberto D* already quoted.

> Curiously, this unfathomable conception of cinematic art reaches its full expression in none of the moments concerning Umberto Domenico Ferrari – who is the mainstay of the action – but in the sequence in which the pregnant maidservant awakes. Each of her imperceptible, useless yet irremediable actions is a precious expense of life . . . [26]

I have already remarked on the importance of indirection in Márquez' *œuvre* at large. It is significant that the most directly political of these three early novellas is the one in which narrative indirection, the use of the lampoons, should also be most overt and strategic. The lampoons are a collective psychological symptom expressing a condition of which the mayor is a part. And as an ambiguously metafictional device, they have some further resonances.

In their malevolence, the lampoons are a development of the anonymous note attached to the doctor's door in *Leaf Storm*. Yet in so far as they arise from a frustrated impulse to tell the truth, they are also a development of the clandestine news sheets of *No One Writes*. In a world of censorship and public lies, the lampoons are a perverted form of truth-telling. It is as if the destructiveness imposed on communal and individual life is internalised as a collective self-destruction. The destructiveness and the truth telling of the lampoons are obscurely mingled and the mystery of their authorship prevents our rationalisng out the two strands of motive. In so far as they are a literary *deus ex machina*, they are less an expression of personal malevolence and more of a Momus glass; a magical revelation of what is normally veiled. This revelatory, and supra-personal, purpose of the lampoons suggests both a journalistic impulse and the magical omniscience of fiction.

When Mr Carmichael seeks to silence the barber's political conversation by saying 'Eso es literatura de periódico' / 'That's just newspaper stories', the barber replies, without denying the charge, 'Es que uno está que revienta por hablar' / 'It's just that one is bursting to talk'.[27] There is an almost biological need to speak out. This relates to journalism, not in the sense of telling people what they don't know so much as in the sense of public self-recognition. There is a need to have what is universally known publicly said, acknowledged. The mayor's final denial of the castration which everyone knows to have taken place enforces the difference between knowing and saying. He is not concerned with what anyone believes but simply with what is to be said. He is 'saving the appearances' in the most cynical modern sense. The barber distributes clandestine news and political commentary as a benign, if dangerous, expression of the need to recognise the truth. Whatever the risks, perhaps it keeps him sane. For it is as if the general strain of living with untruth, although it can apparently be managed from day to day, causes some deep psychic disorder such as is manifest in the lampoons.

In a whimsical article of August 1954 Márquez alluded to the universal human need to spread, and listen to, news. As he develops his theme, his comic fable about journalism begins to suggests an underlying commonality.

> Doubtless the first sensational news ever produced – after the creation – was the expulsion of Adam and Eve from paradise. It must have been an unforgettable first page: ADAM AND EVE EXPELLED FROM PARADISE (over eight columns) . . .
>
> How many years is it since that news appeared? It is as difficult to answer that question as it is to predict when will come the moment to write that last great, sensational report: the last judgement . . . But before that time comes, who knows how many changes journalism will undergo, this burdensome activity which began when one neighbour recounted to another what a third did the previous night. This activity has a curious variant in our small towns where a man who reads the newspapers every day will comment in writing on the news in an article with an unequivocally editorial tone . . .

*   *   *

This commentator on daily life, who can be found in at least forty five per cent of our towns, is a journalist without a paper, a man who exercises his profession despite the hard and unchangeable circumstance of not having even a hand press on which to express his ideas and who therefore expresses them on the public street and does so with such evident results as to provide incontrovertible proof that journalism is a biological necessity of man which for that reason is able to survive even the newspapers themselves . . . [28]

The playful fiction of the article enables Márquez to bring together some favourite themes: notably biblical myths and journalism. The whimsical tone is also a way of suggesting an ineradicable, universal impulse underlying the more formalised activity of the journalist. At this less differentiated level we feel such amateur journalism to have a common root with gossip as one of the necessary expressions of human community. Something of this 'biological necessity' seems implied in the barber's 'bursting to talk'.

This fundamental impulse underlying journalism equally underlies fiction although this likewise has become formally distinct. The article itself is a fable. So too, through the gossip and lampoon theme, Márquez seems subliminally to suggest that journalism and fiction are distinct manifestations of the same underlying human necessity. And fiction, as in this article, is an enabling, speculative frame as much as it is the expression of any specific body of material. It is the general capacity for speculative imaginative premises rather than a particular topic bound by an immediate external occasion.

This may be why, when Dr Giraldo and his wife spend an afternoon reading Dickens, itself a form of retreat from political horror, they embark on a brief discussion of whether it is 'un cuento largo' (p. 91) / 'a long tale' (p. 86) or 'una novela corta' / 'a short novel'. The exchange seems to have little narrative function other than to refer out to the text of *In Evil Hour* itself. And the self-reference is echoed in the doctor's later conversation with Don Sabas who sees the lampoons themselves as a 'novel' for which he is awaiting the resolution. (p. 93/p. 88) Judge Arcadio similarly remarks that the whole affair of the lampoons is 'como leer a novelas policíacas' (p. 108)/ 'like reading detective stories' (p. 104).

In themselves, these fictional self-allusions remain rather puzzling.[29] Márquez seems to be promoting a consciousness of the fiction as fiction at once inseparable, and yet distinct from, the lives of the characters. This is not a metafictional exposure of the characters as fictional beings, and indeed it is hard to say what real purpose is served by this secondary level of recognition. It seems an intuitive, almost compelling, impulse on Márquez' part constantly to hint at a metafictional awareness within the story. It is as if the question of fiction continues to exercise him and to do so specifically within the field of significances generated by the lampoons. At the level of the characters, perhaps, there is a homely recognition of fiction both as an escape and as a mode of understanding; as an angle on experience. But that is a rather minimal significance. Beyond that, the lampoons and the fictional self-awareness seem to have some half-conscious mutual affinity. I take it this is because the lampoons are a malevolent, perverted inflection of the human interest in others for which gossip, journalism and fiction are all distinct manifestations. The common root, and the distinct formal purposes, are a lurking, subtextual concern.

Marquez appears to have had a deep creative sensitivity to the common roots of journalism and fiction. And that is why, despite the close connection between his early fiction and his long and impressive career as a journalist, he never seems in danger of confusing the two activities. His journalism employs all his skills of style and narrative while his fiction is informed by the political and social consciousness of a journalist who has investigated the workings of national and international politics at first hand. But when the two bodies of work are compared, what is most striking is the clear sense of two distinctive modes.

It may well be that Márquez' journalism had a double value in forming the novelist. While, most obviously, giving him his knowledge and exercising a range of expressive and narrative skills, it also freed him from journalistic burdens so as to release the novelist. His article on the novel of *La Violencia* should be understood in this spirit as expressing his own, rather special, need to distinguish the two activities while the uncertain provenance of the lampoons as either naturalistic or metafictional reflects their ambivalent expression of an impulse lying below this formal differentiation.

Once again, the story is a fundamentally naturalistic narrative which, without quite disrupting its own convention, seems to incorporate a sub-textual concern for its own imaginative origins and mode of meaning. There is, even in this early political fiction of Márquez, a persistent, half-submerged meditation on the relationship of fiction to life: a desire to justify it distinctly, but not separably, from journalistic or political purpose. It follows that such a concern is not expressed in a formal self-consciousness of the kind that would merely undermine the realistic force of the fiction for the sake of a stale paradox. It seems rather to be an emergent aspect of the narrative, indeed of the very subject-matter. This implicit, and perhaps largely unconscious, preoccupation of the early fiction helps to explain the sudden creative burst that produced *One Hundred Years of Solitude*.

4

The Cervantean Turn: *One Hundred Years of Solitude*

While seeking to make a living in the Mexican film industry, Márquez suddenly found himself creatively possessed by the theme which he had been contemplating since his earliest days as a writer. His old idea for a novel called *La Casa* (*The House*) now developed into the historical and family saga *One Hundred Years of Solitude*. The sub-textual concerns of his early fiction go some way to explaining this sudden inspiration.

The novel gives a synoptic account of Colombian and more generally Latin American historical experience through the story of the Buendía family. The original couple, José Arcadio Buendía and his cousin Ursula Iguarán, delay the consummation of their marriage because of her fear of incest. When their neighbour, Prudencio Aguilar, imprudently remarks on this situation, José Arcadio kills him and the couple go off with a group of young neighbours to found the town of Macondo. Following an initial 'arcadian' period of seclusion from historical experience under the governorship of their young founder, the people of Macondo suffer an increasing decadence and are obliged to participate in the archetypal events and disillusions of Latin American history from colonial to neo-colonial times.

The opening complex of violence and incest, an emotional frustration arising from the deep-seated emotional solipsism of the Buendías, continues to work out its consequences. Only at the very end, as the town is being destroyed by a great wind, one of several biblical plagues in the narrative, does the last of the Buendías realise that the whole cycle of the town's rise and fall has been foretold in the parchments of the Gipsy, Melquíades.

The revelation of Melquíades' prophetic chronicle raises, or focuses, the crucial questions of interpretation. It reaffirms, what has been evident throughout, that the novel has achieved its synoptic range by a departure from historical realism for the more symbolic mode that has come to be known as 'magical realism'. This makes it difficult to judge how far the whole experience is to be understood as an historical analysis or through the apparent determinism of Melquíades' foretelling. Like the Buendías themselves, the novel is hermetically closed in on itself albeit in a self-conscious and crafted way. Within the world of the novel, further enclosed by the dead-pan humour of the narrative voice, all the basic elements of violence, sexuality, incest and solitude are highly ambivalent. It has proved hard to distinguish tragedy and farce, critique and affection, idealism and illusion in the overall impact of the Buendías' story. To some extent, Márquez' mode of magical realism is a Latin American equivalent of the North American tall tale. We are never quite sure how seriously to take it.

The book has already been the subject of many excellent close readings, most of which attempt to give it a specific interpretation. I think it is most helpful now to stand back and see it more contextually within Márquez' *œuvre* and in relation to other works of modern fiction. In this larger context it becomes clearer why it is a work, like Kafka's novels, specifically designed both to invite and to resist interpretation.

Critics writing while still relatively close to the publication of *Hundred Years* found it natural to stress the partly unconscious teleology by which this work grew from the earlier fiction. But with the retrospect of several later and substantial novels of a different kind it is apparent that *Hundred Years* is at once deeply representative and highly untypical. It indeed grew out of the earlier fiction, and provided an important groundwork for the later fiction, but its representativeness is intimately bound up with its *un*typicality; on its having indeed grown *out* of the *œuvre*. In some ways it is even a reaction against it.

It is important to stress this since the enormous popularity of *Hundred Years* has strongly governed the image of Márquez' fiction at large. That in turn may partly explain his own slightly deprecating attitude towards the novel and his stated preference for other works such as *No One Writes* and *Chronicle of a Death Foretold*. Furthermore, *Hundred Years* is fatally imitable, or rather gives a fatally misleading impression of being so. The mode known as 'magical realism' has aroused, along with its immense popularity, a reaction against what some see as its too-easy recipe book of devices.

This response has been memorably encapsulated by the uptight narrator, and Flaubert fan, of Julian Barnes' *Flaubert's Parrot*, and there seems some danger of Edward Braithwaite's words providing a label to be hung permanently around Márquez' neck:

> Ah, the propinquity of cheap life and expensive principles, of religion and banditry, of surprising honour and random cruelty. Ah, the daiquiri bird which incubates its eggs on the wing; ah, the fredonna tree whose roots grow at the tips of its branches, and whose fibres assist the hunchback to impregnate by telepathy the haughty wife of the hacienda owner; ah, the opera house now overgrown by jungle. Permit me to rap on the table and murmur 'Pass!' [1]

This response is not necessarily Barnes' own, and even his narrator is not strictly thinking of highly original works such as *Hundred Years* so much as the subsequent literary fashion. But it undoubtedly expresses a common response which Barnes has usefully identified with the Flaubertian spirit. That is a theme to develop in connection with Márquez' later fiction. In the immediate context of *Hundred Years*, it is worth noting first that this response points to a real danger for Márquez. He has wisely avoided repeating the mode of *Hundred Years* which might well have led to a sterile self-imitation. But more importantly, he only needed to do it once. It represents a necessary moment in his creative evolution.

To appreciate the force of this point, it is useful first to look more closely at the features which have attracted, for better or worse, the term 'magical realism'. It is not the meaning of the term in itself that matters here but the underlying questions it implies. In other words, I want to look not so much *at* the term as *behind* it. Two critics especially, writing in the early 1970s, have brought out the gradual development of the imaginative mode of *Hundred Years* throughout the earlier works.

Robert Sims has concentrated on the various devices, such as Faulknerian flashbacks, by which the experience of time is spatialised and compacted.[2] This provides the narrative structure through which mythic repetition, the constant re-enactment of past experience in the present, can be dramatically 'present'ed. But Sims's careful study of technique is perhaps too ready to assume that any such spatialisation of time is to be associated with the mythic time sense. Such structures can also express forms of emotional obsession and fixation for which myth is a misleading term and this distinction is very relevant to Márquez. In the event, Márquez' use of such narrative structures continues in his later works without their necessarily invoking the mythic configurations of *Hundred Years* and nor do they always have such a significance even in this novel. Some of these questions will be taken up later, but the issue of the special fictional world is put more radically by the second critic.

In Mario Vargas Llosa's *Gabriel García Márquez: historia de un deicidio* there is a similar assumption that *Hundred Years* is the viewpoint from which to see Márquez' *œuvre*.[3] This excellent reading of Márquez by the Peruvian novelist who was at that time also a friend exemplifies the way Latin American authors have frequently been the best commentators on their fellow writers. Yet the study is also partly taken over by its leading idea: that all writers of fiction, and pre-eminently so in Márquez' case, seek to oust God by creating their own substitute worlds. Accordingly, Vargas Llosa traces the gradual foregrounding in the early fiction of what he calls 'lo real sujetivo' (subjective reality) until by the time of the short story 'Big Mama's Funeral' the whole narrative gets to be subsumed into the subjective. From having elements of fantasy within a naturalistic narrative we move to a narrative form in which the very distinction begins to be elided.

This account is very fair but the central phrase 'subjective reality', like its sister expression 'magical realism', constantly lends itself to a sentimental blankness; if not in Vargas Llosa's own hands then as soon as it leaves them. Above all, the very phrase implicitly acquiesces in the Cartesian dualism which Márquez' literary form is seeking to challenge. It is worth pausing on this philosophical question underlying the literary form.

i. Insomnia Precedes Amnesia

The Cuban novelist Alejo Carpentier, who lived in Paris from 1928 to 1939, consciously adapted the Parisian anti-rationalist movement of surrealism to express a specifically Latin American experience. In a famous essay, he argued that whereas surrealism in Europe was a partial and oppositional movement, it was actually the most appropriate form in which to express Latin American landscape and historical experience.[4] This claim is fraught with problems but it undoubtedly points to an important creative intuition for many Latin American writers. In part, the problem was that surrealism as an art movement was less weighty than some of its underlying principles or insights. Jacques Gilard has remarked how surrealism, in being conceived so much as a movement of cultural opposition, was effectively part of the Cartesian rationalist order to which it was notionally opposed.[5] Some kinds of opposition are really a way of supporting the given order.

The truer influence of surrealism for Latin American writers lay in their assimilation of these underlying insights in such a way as to transform realism rather than oppose it. It is a happy accident that the 'sur' of surrealism in French should mean 'above' while the Spanish 'sur' means south. For the highly conceptual, self-conscious European movement became in Latin America a downward exploration of a psychic frontier as in Borges' favourite story 'El Sur' (The South).[6] Borges' story is a dream within a dream and answers to one of the stronger moments in Andre Breton's surrealist manifesto in which he speaks of the importance of dream experience psychologically and therefore artistically.[7] So too, Márquez' narrative play with conflicting orders of truth and wisdom creates a subtle disturbance which does not discard our modern rationalist culture nor claim access to a superior one. Instead, it gestures forcefully to important limitations and to their largely unwitting consequences. His synoptic invocation of several centuries of modern history suggests the inclusive nature of his critique of the emotional consequences of the Cartesian split of mind and body, or self and world. The critique is not original but, given the emotional and subliminal nature of the problem, it needs constantly to be mounted in fresh ways.

Márquez's special achievement was to find a comic, popular and local mode for this serious critical purpose. His art is to do it imaginatively rather than analytically and as an aspect of a more external historical theme. Márquez' novel conflates into the story of several generations a much longer period of historical experience extending back to a founding myth. The effect is to suggest the continued impact of historical and pre-historical experience in the psyche of the present. Within this compacted psychic structure of *Hundred Years*, the shift from the 'Arcadian' pre-historical era into historical time is figured by the first of the 'biblical' plagues, the memory sickness, which leads in turn to the need to start creating an historical record. The comically Adamic overtones whereby the people of Macondo now have to point at everyday objects since they have forgotten the names of things, leads us to associate the beginning of their history with a re-enactment of the original fall of man. Like some major philosophers, Márquez interprets the mythic Fall from Eden as the cultural fall into dualism; or more precisely the twin dualisms of self versus world and mind versus body. For what has not been sufficiently remarked in the Buendías' shift from Arcadia to history is the fact that the memory loss arises from lack of sleep. They lose the capacity for a recuperative rest from consciousness. In other words, insomnia precedes amnesia and, properly understood, this constitutes a challenge to the well-known philosophical adage of Márquez' own Parisian days, which were the existentialist 1950s rather than the surrealist 1920s, namely the Sartrean formula that 'existence precedes essence'.

Appropriately, the memory sickness, like the pox, is a result of conquest. In the compacted symbolic history of the novel, the disease is rightly caught from the Indian servants since the destruction of someone else's cultural memory usually involves the guilty repression of your own. But the Indians' very form of memory may also have been different from that of their conquerors in being more obviously related to the world of sleep and dream. When the people of Macondo are first told they have the insomnia plague they are more pleased than appalled since they now expect to have more time for their daily activities. But the loss of the apparently useless hours of sleep eventually impairs their capacity to perform even the most necessary functions of everyday life. The daytime self is unwittingly dependent on the night-time self, not just as a period of rest but as an opening to a different order of time and meaning through which the daytime activity itself ultimately needs to be understood.

In other words, the relation of memory and sleep in the double disease suggests that there may be different kinds of memory. There is a rough analogy here with the distinction Proust drew in the personal realm between conscious intentional memory, which is often fallacious, and the unwitting emotional memory that is triggered by chance events and which wells up as a fresh emotional experience in the present. Indeed, the narrator's way of expressing Fernanda's failure to find her wedding ring, has in itself a Proustian ring: ' . . . sin saber que la búsqueda de las cosas perdidas está entorpecida por los hábitos rutinarios . . . '8 / ' . . . not knowing that the search for lost things is hindered by habitual routines . . . '9

In the collective domain, this conscious intentional memory may be akin to the professional activity of historians, while affective memory is more like what Walter Benjamin had in mind when he said: 'To articulate the past historically does not mean to recognize it "the way it really was" (Ranke). It means to seize hold of memory as it flashes up at a moment of danger'.[10] Benjamin was thinking here of history not as an academic discipline but as an immediate living resource and one which is not, in its deepest sources, under conscious control. In this respect the distinction fleshes out Nietzsche's insistence that, for healthy and effective action, it is as important to forget as to remember, and forgetting, even more than memory, must be an effect of time rather than will.[11] To put the point in more homely terms, it is commonly recognised that difficult experiences have, as we say, to be 'slept on' for their longer-term impact to be absorbed and thus to be converted into meaning. This cannot be purely a function of the conscious will.

Borges' story of 'Funes the Memorious', which he himself described as a 'gigantic metaphor for insomnia', is an illuminating inverse of the insomnia and memory sickness.[12] Funes is endowed with a total responsiveness to experience and a complete recall of his past. But this causes insomnia and actually incapacitates him for action and even for thinking. The story is, among other things, an ironic reflection on the arbitrariness of realism and it is appropriate that the narrator's own 'inadequate' memory creates an essentially dream figure in Funes for it is indeed only as an 'unrealistic' dream of Borges himself that Funes can exist for us. The story is, therefore, not only a satire on realism but also the implicit vindication of a different mode of fiction. Something comparable can be seen in *Hundred Years*.

It is significant that during the memory sickness, before the people recover their capacity to function, at least apparently, in the world of daily consciousness, the underlying obsessions of the major characters are overtly dominant. José Arcadio thinks remorsefully of Prudencio Aguilar; Aureliano makes a precious object in his workshop, and Rebeca dreams of her parents. All the characters find themselves, at this time, 'todo el día soñando despiertos' (p. 120) / 'in a waking dream all day' (p. 44). They believe they have been rescued from this state when Melquíades' potion restores their daytime memory. But in truth they have now lost their capacity properly to inhabit both worlds so that the dream world of their suppressed obsessions henceforth imposes itself on their daytime lives. And Melquíades, who like the great epic heroes has himself visited the world of the dead, now retires to chronicle the working out of the Buendias' unconscious destiny in a language they cannot understand.

In the subsequent story of the Buendías it becomes evident that they have lost their proper access to this other realm of sleep; a realm which is commonly expressed, within the terms of daytime consciousness, through magical and dream images. But the fundamental narrative trick of the book, as fundamental as Alonso Quijano's imagining himself as the fictional character, Don Quixote, is that Márquez goes on to tell their story at the level of the Buendías' repressed selves. The inseparability of the two realms is embodied in the narrative mode as the magical dimension of the narrative enacts the structures of which they are not aware. As will be seen in more detail, the narrative adopts a humorous convention of treating the characters' emotions as physical elements and events in the world, so that they, and we, actually see the magical events and elements, but their awareness is more that of sleep-walkers. Their actions in the daytime world are governed by deep structures within which their conscious world, and our narrative world, remain enclosed.

Several times a character is actually described as being 'like a sleepwalker'. This has usually a Quixotic and partly comic implication although it is pathetic in the eventual case of Meme, who wishes to break out of the emotional enclosure of the Buendías and is shocked into a state of sleepwalking trauma, the extreme form of fixated dream, by Fernanda. The implication is that the dream self needs expression and, if its unconscious working is in sleep, its more conscious arena is the imagination. The relation of dream and fiction is unwittingly recognised by the townsfolk as they seek to recover the world of dream by telling themselves the circular story of the capon. Unfortunately, they see this in a simply utilitarian light as a means of exhaustion and miss the deeper instinct which suggests that a story may indeed be the royal road to the realm of the unconscious. Fiction deals importantly with reality but through the dream as well as the daytime self. For Márquez, no less than Borges, a fiction which merely imitates the daily world is itself an empty, and potentially damaging, illusion.

It is useful to see the magical dimension of the story in this way as it helps avoid the more sentimental and dualistic readings to which the narrative has proved susceptible and distinguishes the aspect of psychic projection in the characters from the expressive significance of the narrative mode itself. For magic is ultimately, and most importantly, the chosen mode of the author, Márquez. That is to say, a participation in the Buendías' condition becomes the narrative technique of the book.

This double function creates much of the ambivalence of the narrative. For if the method has a critical implication for the characters, what are we to make of the author's own use of magical projection? The crucial point here is that Márquez' own encompassing insights into the unconscious realm occur under the sign of fiction. Nietzsche, who classically presented the modern anti-dualist critique of Western culture, had some relevant remarks on the artistic use of 'miracles':

> Whoever wishes to test rigorously to what extent he himself is related to the true aesthetic listener or belongs to the community of the Socratic-critical persons needs only to examine sincerely the feeling with which he accepts miracles represented on the stage: whether he feels his historical sense, which insists on strict psychological causality, insulted by them, whether he makes a benevolent concession and admits the miracle as a phenomenon intelligible to childhood but alien to him, or whether he experiences anything else. For in this way he will be able to determine to what extent he is capable of understanding *myth* as a concentrated image of the world that, as a condensation of phenomena, cannot dispense with miracles. It is probable, however, that almost everyone, upon close examination, finds that the critical-historical spirit of our culture has so affected him that he can only make the former existence of myth credible to himself by means of scholarship, through intermediary abstractions.[13]

The reader is not called upon literally to believe in miracles but to respond to them, within the fiction, with a proper aesthetic sympathy. Indeed, for Nietzsche they are an indispensable way of defining that proper sympathy. His remarks catch the humorously disarming, yet challenging, implication of the miraculous in Márquez. For Márquez too has a way of significantly dividing his readers.

On each side of this aesthetic sympathy for *Hundred Years* there lie the two complementary responses which, in their different ways, flatten the effect. One commonly expressed, apparently approving, reaction, which arises in a slightly vulgarised way from Alejo Carpentier, is that Latin American 'reality' is itself magical. This rather collapses the literary effect created with such care by a work such as *Hundred*

Years and it should be said that many Latin Americans, such as Angel Rama, would in any case wish to distance themselves from the note of literary tourism this response implies.[14] The opposite response is the rationalist which, like Julian Barnes' narrator, finds merely hokum in the magical elements. What is really at stake is a psychological suppleness which is able to inhabit unsentimentally the daytime world while remaining open to the promptings of those domains which modern culture has, by its own inner logic, necessarily marginalised or repressed.

The effective meaning of this is caught in a conversation between Márquez and his old friend Plineo Apuleyo Mendoza.[15] When asked directly, Márquez admits to being superstitious and gives instances of his premonitions of future events. However, as he goes on to discuss the particular case of the military coup in Caracas where he had felt the imminence of some important event while out walking with Mendoza, his subsequent explanation is far from superstitious. He suggests that he may have heard military aircraft in the night in some half-waking, unremembered interval between sleep. What he is really talking about is a holistic responsiveness whereby his consciousness is open to such promptings. Such a capacity to foretell events is, of course, highly developed in Colonel Aureliano Buendía in his younger years.

Within our culture the language of superstition may well be the only language available for speaking of this; or it may be the most appropriate language in so far as it asserts a conscious counter-current to the main drift of the culture. It resists the experience being rationalised away. And it is worth remarking in passing, with reference to *Hundred Years* and the insomnia sickness, that Márquez sees his moment of responsiveness as having occurred while half asleep. For the important point is that this capacity does not suggest an either/or choice between rationalism and irrationalism. The daytime world is not an alternative to, nor separable from, this more rounded response. So too, in the same conversation, Márquez acknowledges that the critic Ernesto Volkening was right to detect in him a general view of women as being more whole than men.[16] But he expresses regret that Volkening, by saying so, has made this attitude self-conscious. Márquez does not want everything dragged into the light of daytime consciousness where its meaning and function in the whole economy of the psyche will be changed.

That is why the narrative formula 'insomnia precedes amnesia'

constitutes a challenge to the philosophical formula 'existence precedes essence'. Sartrean existentialism privileged the critical function
of consciousness and denied the value, and even the existence, of
the unconscious domain. Márquez, by contrast, affirms the crucial
importance of the unconscious and avoids the dualistic choice. His
narrative mode embodies the difficult necessity of relating them
without allowing either to dominate.

An important part of Márquez' achievement in *Hundred Years* was
to communicate all this with an appropriate, and popularly accessible, implicitness by simply having the reader share the characters'
experience. Márquez does not drag experience into inappropriate
consciousness in his narrative any more than in his personal life.
Furthermore, the magical dimension of his own tale is able to bring
out the condition of the Buendías while placing the narrative itself
on a human footing with them. He himself has remarked that
critics have generally missed his affection for, and solidarity with,
his characters. This may be partly because the authorial relationship
is not directly embodied in a personalised narrative voice but arises
more intrinsically from the nature of the narrative mode. That is to
say, even while seeing how his characters are caught within their own
dreamlike obsessions, he himself recuperates the realm of dream and
magic in telling their story. Hence although the recuperation is of
little comfort to them, they after all do not escape or have 'una
segunda oportunidad sobre la tierra (p. 493) / 'a second opportunity
on the earth' (p. 336), his story nonetheless salvages a meaning from
their experience. Furthermore, their peculiar form of psychic somnambulism gives them an heroic function as the necessary vehicles
of our recognitions. In *The Birth of Tragedy*, from which the remarks
on miracles were quoted, Nietzsche also comments that incest and
killing, the two central taboos in *Hundred Years*, as in *Oedipus*, are
associated with the acquiring of prophetic wisdom.[17] In its very
different, deliberately unheroic, manner, the humorous narration
of *Hundred Years* expresses both the underlying human relationship
with the characters and the insight achieved through their delusions
and excesses.

This implicit psychic penetration also arises from the way the
book's serious historical material is presented through a consciously
linguistic lens. Brian McHale has pointed out how its narrative
language constantly equivocates between the literal and the metaphorical so that actual incidents seem to be spawned by metaphor.[18]
McHale cites, among others, the case of Amaranta Ursula who

returns from Europe to Macondo 'llevando al esposo amarrado por el cuello con un cordel de seda' (p. 450) / 'leading her husband by a silk cord tied round his neck' (p. 305). At first, we respond to this as a common metaphorical idea. But later it emerges that the cord is quite literal. This stylistic trick is more than a trick in that it foregrounds the deep-lying metaphors in common speech. George Lakoff and M. Johnson, in *Metaphors We Live By*, have traced some of the largely unwitting clusters of metaphor through which psychological and emotional experience in particular are commonly expressed.[19]

On this view, metaphor is a kind of linguistic unconscious. Although we normally read through it transparently, this buried structure of metaphor does, in some unaccountable measure, shape our world. Márquez changes the focus of his narrative language so as to enlarge and literalise this metaphorical order. He brings the linguistic unconscious to the surface in a way that is disarmingly humorous as well as rendering it both strange and familiar. It is a comic equivalent of Freud's 'uncanny'. In this respect, the old Negro 'cuya cabeza algodonada le daba el aspecto de un negativo de fotografía' (p. 457) / 'whose cottony head gave him the appearance of a photographic negative' (p. 311) is an image of the whole narrative medium. It is a constant reversal by which the elements of external reality become shadowy while psychological structures become concretised. So, for example, Remedios' emotional unavailability and airiness become a literal floating from the world. Or the dead remain visible presences as long as they persist in the emotional memories of the living.

In this way, the book recognises a subliminal domain in human personality while, just like the earlier fiction, avoiding introspection and by-passing a Freudian conception of the unconscious. The concentration on the linguistic plane has further consequences. If deep-lying metaphors structure our common world this means they are dead metaphors, or clichés, which means in turn that they are completely shared, and to call Márquez' narrative mode 'subjective' or 'magical' risks losing much of the point. Language in particular resists the distinction of inner and outer, of subjective and objective. It is a human construction but necessarily a communal, not a private, one. Wittgenstein remarked that men may disagree in their opinions but have to agree in the language they use.[20] The very fact of language embodies a fundamental human solidarity constantly obscured by the level of conflicting opinion or interest.

On a similar principle, Stanley Cavell has very relevantly pointed out how the treatment of slaves was at once an explicit denial of their humanity and an implicit assumption of it.[21] Understanding language in this way has therefore a potentially political, as well as an anti-Cartesian, implication. If language constructs the world, then how is this being done, by whom, and whose world is it anyway? These questions, too, Márquez addresses implicitly within his own play with language.

ii.   Whose World?

I have already suggested that Márquez' narrative mode is an evident, if necessarily elusive, challenge to the rationalism most notably embodied in French culture. It is elusive in that we can more easily see the critique than we can define the positive alternative. This posture underlies a comparable elusiveness with respect to cultural norms more generally. Marquez, like other Latin American writers, saw Paris as the effective cultural capital of the old continent and Jacques Gilard has commented on Márquez' peculiarly balanced and confident attitude to European high culture even when he first went to Paris.[22] Neither awed nor rejecting, he had from the outset a strong sense of the value of who he was and where he came from.

Part of the force of *Hundred Years* is that it addresses the question of provincialism and centrality which had been a constant, if often implicit, preoccupation of his journalism. Metropolitan centres enable a special concentration and rapid transmission of thought but such places also have their dangers. Anyone in the world who troubles to read and think the best that is generally available is not likely in any damaging sense to be provincial and may well have a built in sense of the relativity of cultural horizons. By the same token, it is frequently the conscious inhabitant of the accepted cultural centre who is open to the most insidious and damaging provincialism: the complacent incapacity to imagine anything beyond that horizon. In his journalistic progress from the small coastal town of Barranquilla, through the Colombian capital Bogotá, on to Paris and finally to the Latin American regional purview of *Prensa Latina*, Márquez was constantly riding the multiple ironies of this question. His recognition that he should tell this story in a narrative voice approximating that of his small-town grandmother, who told of marvels as everyday events, suggests the creative breakthrough effected by his appreciation of the 'provincial' viewpoint. It is no accident that the creative significance of his grandmother's voice should have come to him after his culturally mobile career in journalism.

Although I have suggested that a principal value of Márquez' journalism was to save him from putting it into his fiction, this was also to affirm their common roots. His journalism always required a constant adjustment of scale between local and world interests. It was even more evidently part of his function as foreign correspondent to explain external events locally and local events externally. This constant dilation and contraction of the reporter's eye, which is foregrounded in the journalism, underlies the fiction as an implicit sense of scale. Once again, *Hundred Years* is unusual in bringing the question to the thematic surface.

In the journalism, this pervasive awareness is focused in Márquez' repeated use of the word 'world', particularly in the formulaic phrase 'the most . . . in the world'. The phrase is especially revealing because his repeated use of it seems in some measure unconscious, like a verbal tic. The very phrase embodies a constant adjustment of vision and tone, as between humorous appreciation of the provincial and serious awareness of a global or universal scale.

As part of his frequent play with cliché and popular expression, he speaks at one point of Ava Gardner, quoting her publicity notices in ironic quotation marks, as 'the most beautiful animal in the world'.[23] The irony here is directed not at the film star but at the expression itself and at his own adoption of it. The common phrase 'most beautiful girl in the world' is as senseless as it is tasteless when taken literally. Yet it is perfectly comprehensible as an item of popular emotional rhetoric and, of course, it is precisely in its literal absurdity that we recognise its metaphorical truth of feeling. In Márquez, such a use of the formula is always in humorous tension with a spectrum of different uses. The other end of the spectrum can be seen in a remark from a film review: 'The Italians are the second greatest consumers of film in the world'.[24] As a weekly reviewer of films from around the world, and as a journalist commenting on geo-political events for a specific local readership, Márquez makes a perfectly literal reference to a global criterion.

As the same formulaic phrase constantly modifies from the most subjective rhetoric to soberly statistical statement, it puts the two extremes in a constant ironic conjunction. It is a verbal epitome of his constant adjustment of scales. The local and the global, along with the rhetorical and the literal, are, of course, the axes on which the humorous and political viewpoint of *Hundred Years* is built. Márquez' verbal tic reflects the interpenetration of the local and the universal. Any fully human 'world' must surely be both and this may be an important clue to the immense popularity of *Hundred Years* around the world.

Hundred Years tells a highly local story through a universal biblical myth of origins and foundation. Much of the book's charm lies in the interplay of the two aspects. And much of its ambiguous meaning too. Towards the end, the young aspirant writer, Gabriel, escapes the doomed and enclosed world of Macondo to go to Paris. The big interpretative crux of the book is the question of how far its meaning is enclosed in the local text, the foretold history, written in Sanskrit by Melquíades, or is rather to be found in Márquez' Spanish narrative which, through the medium of further translations, passes beyond this local consciousness to a world audience. And, of course, the capacity to foretell the local future was itself a function of Melquíades' universal wisdom put down in a language belonging to a remote history and coming from the other side of the world. As always in *Hundred Years*, each term dissolves into its opposite.

The larger significance of this question can be seen by comparing Márquez' combination of local history and universal myth with some other mythopoeic historical narratives from earlier in the century. In the time of Joyce, Lawrence, Mann, Yeats and Proust the competing nationalisms and imperialisms of Europe came to a point of catastrophic conflict in the Great War. Although all of these writers were strongly imbued with, and sometimes celebrated, the characteristics of their own national cultures, they shared a fundamental critique of nationalism. They also lived in an era when several key formative systems of thought had apparently revealed universal characteristics in human 'nature' and culture. In the inner domain of the psyche, the Freudian revolution stressed the common structures of the unconscious; an implication to be followed even more strongly by Jung. Likewise, the late nineteenth-century anthropology of Frazer and others seemed to have revealed common patterns in the early stages of all human culture. Hence in turning to myth for their narrative structures these authors were, among other things, appealing to universal values transcending national cultures. It is important to remember this critical and liberating impulse in the mythopoeia of the modernist generation *vis-à-vis* European nationalism since, with the passing of their historical moment, their works have frequently acquired, or been accorded, a different meaning. We are now in a position, partly because of the radical achievement of the modernist generation, to see their works as residually Eurocentric in a way that traduces their original spirit and their historical impact.

Since then, new modes of psychological and anthropological thinking have undercut the universalist premises of such mythopoeia. Furthermore, the Fascist co-option of myth as part of its political rhetoric proved largely successful in tainting the very term despite the attempts of Thomas Mann and others to retain it as a humanist value. Hence in the latter half of the century literary use of myth has been predominantly quizzical and deconstructive, or when it is used positively it is only after being carefully bracketed with a sceptical consciousness. The truth value of myth, in other words, is now generally understood to be at best highly relative. Márquez is of this later generation and illuminates the point of tension between the earlier modernist universalism and a later spirit: deconstructive, relativistic and localised. I say a point of tension since Márquez does not merely debunk the universal either. Myths of a universal humanity constantly irradiate his local tale.

Octavio Paz caught something of the same transitional moment in his own way. In using the theme of solitude to define the peculiar historical experience, and resultant psychological configurations, of Latin America, Paz risked indulging the consolatory sentimentalism, that 'charm of the pathetic', which Borges detected in such theories of specialness.[25] But Paz reversed the terms to suggest that the Mexican, in his very peculiarity, had become the potential, or indeed the inevitable, focus of universal interests.

> The old plurality of cultures, postulating various and contrary ideals, and offering various and contrary views of the future, has been replaced by a single civilization and a single future. Until recently, history was a meditation on the many truths proposed by many cultures, and a verification of the radical heterogeneity of every society and archetype. Now history has recovered its unity and become what it was at the beginning: a meditation on mankind. And mankind too has recovered its unity. . . . The decisions we make in Mexico now affect all men, and vice versa. . . . Each man's fate is that of man himself. Therefore, every attempt we make as Mexicans to resolve our conflicts must have universal validity or it will be futile from the outset.[26]

Hundred Years is a striking instance of Paz' general point which it implicitly thematises. For the book constantly superimposes the private world of the Buendías' somnambulistic solipsism, the archetypal structures of myth, and the geo-political world of modern history which we glimpse through this narrative prism.

Yet Paz' words, written in the middle of the century perhaps, assume too readily the effacement of local culture and consciousness; and such an effacement was often an ideological commitment of politically progressive thinking. The latter decades of the century have revealed cultural and local differences to be more deeply rooted than had often been supposed, or than political institutions had generally allowed for; except, of course, for rightist regimes which have deliberately exploited the resulting political vacuum. The importance of writers like Márquez, Carlos Fuentes, Salman Rushdie or Mikhail Bulgakov is to send a complexly regionalised consciousness around the world which political institutions may sooner or later have to learn to reflect. It may be that truly living together on the planet will be a matter not of tolerating, but of celebrating, difference. This is not to be achieved by international touristic culture industries such as Fuentes' has satirised as 'pepsicoatl'.[27] It may rather be reflected in quite different views of what it means to be human as one looks from the vantage point of a different regional history.

It is significant that Márquez grasps all this not at the level of institutions and politics but of sensibility, and especially of popular sensibility. The cosmopolitan tendency within all societies is inevitable and to some extent desirable. But many do not wish to leave home either physically or mentally and it may well be that the proper relation between local popular consciousness and an educated cosmopolitan consciousness is more like that of consciousness and unconsciousness, or waking and sleeping, as figured in the insomnia sickness. Both aspects are necessary although it would be hard to say analytically how they co-exist. Márquez' adoption of his grandmother's voice, and his assimilation of so many local or family experiences in *Hundred Years*, is the enactment of such a combined consciousness. The dangerous nostalgias of the Buendías are differently echoed in the benign nostalgia of the writer, who is able to draw genuine sustenance from this local world precisely because he is no longer simply of it. *Hundred Years* has been generally recognised as expressing the Colombian historical experience assimilated to a regional one. It is the quintessential Latin American history. The apparent naturalness with which it achieves this arises from Márquez' readiness to think simultaneously on these different scales with each acting as an implicit critical check on the other.

These remarks suggest that the popular, as well as the regional, note of *Hundred Years* is an important part of its meaning. Another significant political shift in later twentieth-century fiction, along with the reaction against Eurocentrism, is a rejection of the perceived cultural exclusiveness of modernism. This shift of attitude can be seen crudely and sympomatically in the common use of 'élitism' as a term of would-be abuse. In the period of Joyce, much serious literary expression became technically recondite, and removed from the popular, in a way that had not seemed necessary for George Eliot or Dickens. T. S. Eliot made this point explicitly.[28] Yet the ideological intention of modernist writing was frequently to celebrate the popular. So Joyce, for example, placed the ordinary figure of Bloom at the centre, in evaluative as well as narrative terms, of *Ulysses*. This gap between technique and aspiration often produces a nostalgia at the heart of such works; a nostalgia that surfaces at moments such as the 'pleasant whining of the mandolin' in *The Waste Land*.[29] Certainly, later writers can escape this by slumming, or cocking a snook at high culture, but genuinely to encompass serious expression within a popular form remains a remarkable achievement. When successful, it is a politically pregnant act in itself.

In finding a relationship between the popular and the sophisticated, Márquez modifies both of them although, once again, it is hard to say exactly how. It is worth remembering that Borges saw the falseness of a writer's conscious relation to his tradition as lying not in the fact but in the self-consciousness. A national tradition is either an 'inescapable act of fate' or 'a mere affectation'.[30] The relationship of the sophisticated and the popular, just like that between the local and the universal, properly eludes definition.

iii. History, Fiction and Myth

Elusiveness is indeed the hallmark of this book. When one attempts to grasp it as history, fiction or myth it proves to be structured like a Moebius strip, in which each interpretative surface modulates constantly into its opposite. Most fundamentally, we are obliged to distinguish, but can never separate, Melquíades' foretold narrative from the retrospective one of Márquez' novel. In fiction, historical consciousness is always crucially modified by the literary structure in which it is embodied, but Márquez gives us competing structures for the same story. Yet this is not, as sometimes in Cortázar for example, just for the sake of the metafictional trick itself. The trick in Márquez is load bearing. The force of this for *Hundred Years* can be seen through a brief comparison with several classic works of twentieth-century fiction which individually parallel some of the most important of this novel's interpretative surfaces.

Joyce's *Ulysses*, although pregnant with historical consciousness, used a spatialised mythic structure. His post-symbolist aesthetic enabled him to create a viewpoint transcending immediate historical questions. The stance of the book is comparable to what Nietzsche called the 'superhistorical'.[31] This modernist possibility, classically embodied in Joyce, had a decisive impact on subsequent fiction but does not by any means represent the only modern possibility. Other writers sought to stay within the form of historical realism although often with difficulty as if this form was increasingly unable to contain their whole vision. Such writers, pushing at the limits of historical realism from the inside, are the most illuminating with respect to Márquez. In particular, *Hundred Years* can be flanked by Conrad's *Nostromo* (1904) on the one hand and Lawrence's *The Rainbow* (1915) on the other.

In *Nostromo*, Conrad shows the inevitable corruption of political idealism by the 'material interests' on which it depends. He sets his tale in an imaginary Latin American country suffering the impact of neo-colonial capitalism. He narrates it through a method of flashback which disorients the linear 'progress' of the story and enforces a sense of inevitability as the outcome is known in advance. By contrast, Lawrence, as a younger contemporary of Conrad, saw him as too ready to acquiesce in the deterministic analysis of contemporary history which had been partly enshrined in the literary form of naturalism. Hence, in *The Rainbow*, which was his own first, fully mature attempt to treat synoptically of modern social history, Lawrence challenged this enclosure of sensibility as much as the economic and social vision *per se*.

Our fundamental mode of vision, as implying a radical way of existing in the world, was the true crux of the problem for Lawrence. And so, from within the broad mode of realism, Lawrence sought to push back its frontiers. Hence, in *The Rainbow*, he tells the story of several modern generations of an unusual, but representative, family within whose collective life-span a much longer process of history is compressed. It is compressed most essentially within their individual and collective psyches but it is also expressed in an ultimate myth of origin based on a transformation of the Genesis story. It even has a central female character called Ursula, who embodies the family's positive traits, and in whose name Lawrence recognised a pagan goddess beneath the medieval cult of virginity.[32]

We may usefully think of Conrad and Lawrence as reflecting respectively the 'Melquíades' and the 'Márquez' narratives of *Hundred Years*. Conrad's vision was perhaps too darkly enclosed within its own pessimistic logic while Lawrence's, as he himself came to see, was perhaps too optimistic. The point of invoking them is to see how cunningly, and equivocally, Márquez has interrelated two similar possibilities. The fatalistic historical vision of the chronicle is mediated through a further narrative level, the novel itself, whose humorous tone and mysteriously external provenance constantly belie enclosure within the terms of Melquídes' prophecy.

Both Conrad and Lawrence sought to stay within a broad conception of historical realism. But Márquez' more obvious foregrounding of the fictional form lends significance to the way Lawrence, even by the time of *The Rainbow*, was already straining quite consciously to transcend the terms of realism. At one point he says of his Ursula:

> It pleased her to know, that in the East one must use hyperbole, or else remain unheard; because the Eastern man must see a thing swelling to fill all heaven, or dwindled to a mere nothing, before he is suitably impressed. She immediately sympathized with this Eastern mind.[33]

Lawrence's emphasis here falls not on hyperbole itself, but on Ursula's sympathy for it. So, too, his own narrative does not use hyperbole as a figure of speech but rather creates a hyperbolic dimension within the narrative.[34] Márquez' 'magical realism' is likewise, in its own way, a creation of narrative hyperbole. The hyperbole, that is to say, cannot be isolated as an effect of style because it constitutes the substance of the action. The very events are hyperbolic. For Márquez is also attempting not so much to describe a known world as to expand and enrich the sensibility in which any such 'world' is perceived. It is important to both writers that their fiction not be isolable as mere fantasy. Nor should it, of course, be read too literalistically.

It is also relevant that the radical nature of Lawrence's cultural critique, combined with the frustrations of his reception including

the banning of *The Rainbow*, placed an increasing strain on his use of
the novel form. He went round the world and eventually gravitated
to Latin America to find the place that most embodied his 'world'.
In his Mexican novel, *The Plumed Serpent* (1926), realist form broke
down completely beneath the strain of his political and psychic
speculations.[35] Lawrence's encounter with Mexico, like Carpentier's
co-option of surrealism, suggests at once the importance of a Latin
American or Third World dimension and a radical dissatisfaction
within European culture and consciousness. What is at stake, in
other words, is not a special Latin American 'reality' but the value of
the Third World standpoint in seeing the limitations of a dominant
modern mode of sensibility to be found in the world at large.

Márquez seems to have responded both to the naturalistic determinism which I have exemplified in Conrad and to the mythopoeic
recourse most notably seen in Lawrence. And in the figure of
Melquíades, in his timeless seclusion, we may also see a hint of
the aestheticist transcendence typified by Joyce. Yet none of these
fictional modes, with their corresponding orders of interpretation,
seems definitively to control the meaning of the book. Just as we
can now see much late nineteenth-century naturalist fiction to have
had an emotional fatalism mixed up in it, so Márquez seems to
view all grandly summative attitudes with suspicion. Yet he does
not dismiss them either. He rather keeps all these possibilities in
mutual, and humorous, suspension. But what is remarkable is that
it never feels like a mere fictional game in the mode of Cortazar or
Borges. Neither the humour nor the fictional self reference diminish
its condensed historical impact. Rather than undermining each other
as mere cleverness, the different possibilities throw each other into
relief. It may be that, even apart from Márquez' evident reflection on
the history of the region, his capacity to ride the shifting possibilities
comes also from one of the deepest of his literary historical tap-roots:
Cervantes.

iv. The Cervantean Turn

Hundred Years is an overtly Cervantean book in its fundamental
device of the fictitious foreign historian. But the Cervantean parallel
has a deeper significance with implications for his *œuvre* at large. I
have suggested that *Hundred Years* is Márquez' most substantial and
representative work and yet is also, in important ways, untypical. In

this respect, *Hundred Years* stands in the same relation to Márquez' *œuvre* as *Don Quixote* does to Cervantes' and for essentially similar reasons. If Cervantes had died immediately after completing the second part of *Don Quixote* (1615), or if Márquez had died after *Hundred Years*, their respective *œuvres* would not just be shorter, they would have, or would appear to have, a significantly different meaning.

Cervantes lived at a cultural and literary crossroads. He inherited several distinct modes of fiction which he was able to practise individually with equal skill. He began his career with the pastoral romance *La Galatea* (1585) and died while still working on the comparably idealistic *Persiles and Sigismunda* (1616). Yet over the middle years of his career he wrote a variety of tales, many of them sharply realistic, which are included in the *Exemplary Novels* (1613). It is not surprising, therefore, to find throughout his career a concern for the possible truth values of fiction. The incommensurate modes of fiction in which he thought and wrote brought this concern to the foreground with a pressing urgency. He could see the incipient anachronism and limitation of the romance form to which he was nonetheless most seriously committed. And he could also see the complementary limitation of a cynical, earthbound realism such as he would have found in Mateo Aleman's immensely popular *Guzmán de Alfarache* (1602). The composition of *Don Quixote*, like that of *Hundred Years*, seems to have crept up on the author almost unawares in mid-career and to have expanded into his unexpected *summa* as he found a fictional arena in which his various fictional modes could interact and test each other. To some extent, *Don Quixote*, like *Hundred Years*, was conceived as a kind of sport and has disarmingly preserved something of that character while actually providing the unique arena in which the author has been able to air a complex of questions implicit in his *œuvre* at large. And yet even after writing the second part of *Don Quixote*, Cervantes worked on *Persiles* as his intended masterpiece. Although he saw the popularity, and obviously understood the complexity, of his own achievement, even he was hardly in a position to appreciate its full historical significance. This significance, after all, is partly the story of the novel form itself and the Latin American writers of Márquez' generation constitute one more chapter in its unfolding.

Although Márquez came at the end rather than the beginning of the realist tradition, he was faced with a comparable tension between modes of fiction. He also felt under pressure, as has been seen, to satisfy political demands running counter, but not simply counter, to his own fundamental instincts and convictions about the nature of fiction. Hence, like Cervantes, he found himself in mid-career writing a book in which the underlying, off-stage tensions of his *œuvre* at large had themselves become the thematic centre and the very action of the work. It is not surprising that both authors felt themselves taken over by these central works. One can also see why neither Cervantes nor Márquez felt the need to do it twice and why they might have been inclined in some measure to underestimate the relative achievement. For the work is in each case the tip of an iceberg; it is an impressive eminence sustained by a lifetime's implicit meditation on its themes.

The superimposition of disparate world views as embodied in different fictional genres is the technique that Márquez in his own day shares with Cervantes in his. Their common theme, the projection of psychic obsessions on to the world, provided a sudden transformative significance for the very medium of their fiction. The relation of fiction to life had been the constant, pressing concern behind all of Márquez' previous fiction. When this underlying concern finally found expression as a necessary and explicit part of what he had previously thought of as the historical family saga of *La Casa*, it evidently came as a sudden, transformative charge of creative energy. This central question, so banal when addressed in the abstract, became the most powerful and encompassing theme when it was suddenly instantiated in a concrete and appropriate occasion. That seems to have happened to both Cervantes and Márquez in mid-career and to have produced in each case a work that is the more profoundly representative in its very atypicality.

So too Marquez, like Cervantes, uses the errors of his characters as a way of teaching us how to read the novel. Or more precisely, perhaps, how *not* to read it, for any positive model seems elusive of definition and is only to be approached through the correction of error. In particular, both authors play, time and again, on the fallacy of literalistic reading. I have said that the curious trick of *Hundred Years* is that its characters live out their obsessions in the real world and allow us to do so with them. In literalising metaphor within his fiction, Márquez is reversing the literalism of the Buendías in their actual lives. With Don Quixote, the problem strictly lies not so much in the unreality or anachronism of the models he tries to follow as in the literalism with which he understands them. Likewise, at the beginning of *Hundred Years*, the alchemical sage Melquíades offers an idealistic source of wisdom comparable to the novels of chivalry in Cervantes. The error lies in the literalism with which these essentially symbolic forms of wisdom are assimilated by José Arcadio and Don Quixote. Alchemy betokens a search for perfection which came to be vulgarly understood as the attempt to produce gold from base metal and was then in turn superseded by chemistry in the modern scientific world view. In a sense, the traducing of alchemy to a utilitarian end could be seen not just as the decline of one tradition but as already the beginning of the new in so far as modern scientific reason can no longer claim the ancient association of knowledge with wisdom.

Márquez conflates all three levels in his opening chapter. He contrasts José Arcadio's absurdly literalistic response to Melquíades' knowledge and places both conceptions within a humorous narrative consciousness of the scientific world view shared by the modern author and reader. This establishes the essential mode of the book. For the modern world view is humorously, but not really, displaced. We merely glimpse, comically and obliquely, what for us has to be an incomprehensible association of knowledge, wisdom and power. As in Yeats' poem 'Leda and the Swan' this conjunction falls outside of historical time and experience. José Arcadio's utilitarian and literalistic response is only a parodically extreme version of our own culture in this respect.[36] The alchemical allusions thus provide an oblique comment on the inadequacy of our own cultural terms without in themselves needing to be a matter of literal 'belief' any more than Nietzsche thought miracles must be.

The original gypsies, who seem still in touch with some tradition of esoteric knowledge and power, are soon replaced by a band of pure tricksters and the folk memory of this ambivalent tradition persists in Macondo as part of the book's running commentary on its own mode of meaning. The daguerrotype, photograph and film are successive modern techniques of imitation in which a lifelike image can be produced mechanically without artistic skill or significance. Hence when the people of Macondo encounter Bruno Crespi's cinema they see it as another trick of the gypsies and reject it as 'una máquina de ilusión' / 'an illusion machine' (p. 300) whereby 'nadie podía saber a ciencia cierta dónde estaban los límites de la realidad' (p. 301) / 'nobody could know for sure where were the limits of reality' (p. 186). They cannot accept that their tears for the death of a personage one week can be followed by the same 'person' returning in different dress a week later. Behind their comically inappropriate response there lies a further irony reminiscent of the episode in which Don Quixote breaks up Master Pedro's puppet show.[37] For the inappropriate literalism of these responses actually reflects an empty and mechanical illusionism in both the film and the puppet show. At a deeper level the response *is* appropriate. By contrast, the source of true wisdom in *Hundred Years* is either Melquíades' chronicle, which requires dedication to decipher, or else Márquez' own magical and involuted fiction, which is a puzzle to read.

Neither Cervantes nor Márquez seem to propose answers so much as an education in living with a complex consciousness. Of course, what pass for 'answers' in this domain are often emptily abstract substitutes for understanding. Thus in the fundamental structure of both books the device of the fictitious historian presents us with an irresolvable logical conundrum; as irresolvable as the alogical relation of art to life on which it encourages us to meditate. But the open-endedness of the structure reacts in a constantly fresh way with its specific content. Above all, this Cervantean structure of concentrated meditation is brought to bear upon Márquez' sense of a modern and a regional history.

The different historical moments of Cervantes and Márquez are reflected in their different uses of the fictitious historian device. Cervantes was writing at a time when the modern senses of history and fiction were still hardly differentiated within their common nexus of moral exemplum such as we may still see in Shakespeare's history plays. Accordingly, he exploits the idea of history to affirm the independent 'truth' of fiction. Márquez, on the other hand, writes fiction to assert an historical memory which had already proved vulnerable to the forces of history itself. The book contains two important complexes of historical reference, each of which qualifies the other. The massacre of the strikers is a real historical event preserved in the memory of Márquez' fiction even as that fiction traces its suppression in official historical memory. The other important body of direct historical reference is the literary group, including 'Gabriel' and the Catalan sage, who befriend the last Aureliano. These provide a growing point which extends beyond both Melquíades' chronicle and Márquez' text. Where Cervantes in his day used the idea of history to justify fiction, Márquez in his time uses fiction to preserve an essential history.

At the same time, Márquez' fiction is a defence against the cruder demands of history. His formative years were still those in which writers of a politically progressive stance felt the pressure to be politically 'committed', in Sartre's rather narrow and literalistic sense. Over the course of the 1960s and after, the period in which vulgar Marxism was superseded by the new left, a more subtle pressure has been put, not just on writing, but also on the perceived significance of literature at large. This is the view espoused most notably in Fredric Jameson's *The Political Unconscious*, whereby all fiction, and all experience, is ultimately political, although often unconsciously so.[38] On this account, it is then the function of critical readers to bring the political unconscious of the fiction to the surface. Jameson, I would say, is taking an important, but familiar, truth and expanding it into a populist falsehood. It is true that all experience, and therefore all fiction, is political. It does not follow, however, that politics provides the ultimate horizon of significance for all human life and actions. There are complex questions here, of course, which is why one can always play to the gallery with fashionable half-truths. Márquez' use of the fictitious historian, the solitary and enigmatic sage, Melquíades, is an emblematic affirmation of the opposite truth. Although everything is indeed political, politics cannot instruct us on the purposes and values of human life. Marquez is far from being anti-political but he resists the half truths which often have to underlie political action, and affirms the importance of self-knowledge, the contact with the dream self, which remains a *sine qua non* of individual and collective life.

Whether or not he was responding to this general pressure that Jameson has more recently embodied, Márquez uses his Cervantean structure to hold the radical question constantly before our eyes: the distinction and yet inseparability of fictive and historical 'truth'. The great early modern writers such as Joyce, Lawrence and Thomas Mann assimilated history and fiction into a Nietzschean understanding of myth. For them, the human horizon is necessarily a cultural construction but one within which human beings can nonetheless only live if they have an enabling faith. Healthy life and action require an existential trust in the world. Hence the high modernist mythopoeia expressed, in its fundamental structure and metaphysic, a consciously constructed world within which the characters nonetheless behaved with an intuitive acceptance of their reality.[39] This is the serious recognition underlying the modernist use of 'simple' figures such as Leopold Bloom and Hans Castorp.

But in many ways this self-conscious mythopoeia enabled a traditional humanist conception to continue on a new metaphysical basis, much as ancient buildings are given a new modern structure from the inside while preserving their character and façade. As this mythopoeic inheritance passed to Márquez' generation, however, and to non-European writers, there was an increasing suspicion of its recuperative and potentially mystifying posture. Márquez' own imagination, after all, seems to have been fired by the bottomless scepticism of Kafka rather than the high modernist syntheses of Joyce or Mann. Yet in his own way he also wishes to effect a positive synthesis. Literature may well be 'el mejor juguete que se había inventado para burlarse de la gente' (p. 462) / ' the best plaything ever invented for making fools of people' (p. 314) but it is also a supreme, and uniquely holistic, form of understanding. Hence in Márquez' synthetic structure the different elements of fiction and history are visible even as they are inseparably interwoven. The threads remain distinct while the cloth is whole.

Márquez' Cervantean structure is crucial to this multiple meaning. It keeps these threads separate; it enforces their unresolvable relation at any abstract or general level; and it nonetheless communicates a positive vision of their combined meaning. Literature can communicate its understanding of life because it is not life. Cervantes justified a literature of entertainment with the apparently modest remark that 'the bow cannot always be bent'. But if one ponders his image one recognises that a bow which *was* always bent would actually lose its spring. The relaxation is integral to its proper functioning. One might say something comparable of the human psyche while, of course, allowing for its being a much more complex affair. In the human case, for example, it might be desirable to distinguish different forms of relaxation.

v. Solitude and Solidarity

All this helps to explain why *Hundred Years* is, in several senses, a hermetic book. It invokes the secret lore of alchemy to suggest an ideal association of knowledge and power with wisdom. But just as this can only be glimpsed in a form incomprehensible to our culture, so the book is hermetically sealed in on itself at the level of its narrative logic. At the same time, the effects of fiction are not fully contained by logic. As in Primo Levi's *The Periodic Table* (1975), we see fiction to be a kind of alchemy whereby experience is turned into meaning. By enclosing his historical material within an overt and jokey fiction, Márquez has actually made that history available

to understanding, and particularly to emotional understanding, in a
new way and in a form which is at once popular and subliminal.

At one level, he presents a synoptic vision of regional history in
the light of deep emotional structures. All readers sense its fatalistic
momentum. Yet the fatalism is of the characters as much as in the
'external' events. Fatalism rather than fate is their problem. In this
sense we stand outside it and can see the whole hundred-year cycle
as a process that is now hermetically sealed into an historical, comic,
bitter and nostalgic story. The whole action is being consigned to
the past. Where Joyce's autobiographical Stephen Dedalus wished
to 'awake' from the 'nightmare' of history, Márquez shows Gabriel
actually escaping from the somnambulism of the Buendías.[40]

Virtually all commentators have remarked on Cervantes' ambivalence towards the chivalric romances which he was ostensibly
satirising in *Don Quixote*. As Borges notes, it was his nostalgia *for*
these tales which actually powered his narrative.[41] Profiting from
Cervantes' example, Márquez has built a similar ambivalence into
his tale more consciously and thematically. The nostalgia which is
the besetting sin of the Buendías is the powerful, but critically
self-conscious, emotion of the narrative; the Buendías being, of
course, the vehicles both of the nostalgia and of its critique. When
Márquez' Nobel prize acceptance speech reversed the ending of
Hundred Years to affirm that 'the lineal generations of one hundred
years of solitude will have at last and forever a second chance
on the earth' he was only making explicit the reversibility of
terms which constantly characterises the overall structure and the
individual themes of *Hundred Years*.[42] Just as Cervantes saw that the
cautionary *tale* of the *im*pertinent curiosity was most appropriately
listened to out of curiosity, so the nostalgic psychology of the
Buendías will be best understood through a nostalgic narrative.[43]
What gives the jokey formal circularity of *Hundred Years* its deeper
life is its appropriateness to this complex structure of feeling. The
jokiness partly disguises the deeper feeling while more subliminally
focusing it.

This is also why the apparently conflicting readings of *Hundred
Years* have arisen at the more consciously interpretative level as
people have tried to make intellectually tidy sense of it or have used
it to support their own preferred emphases. But, more subliminally
and intuitively, readers seem constantly to respond to the deeper
and more complex emotional experience of the book. Gramsci
spoke of the pessimism of the intellect needing to be counteracted

by optimism of the will. By mediating the pessimistic narrative of Melquíades through the Cervantean humour of his own novel, Márquez suggests something beyond Gramsci's politically conceived alternatives.

What this 'something' might actually be, as defined in the abstract, remains hard to say, but the thrust of the book is to suggest that it should indeed remain elusive. Márquez seems to embody this recognition in the figure of Melquíades. In the double enclosure of the inner room and the incomprehensible parchments, Melquíades focuses the ambivalence of the narrative structure and of the central term 'solitude'. For solitude seems not an entirely bad thing for Márquez; as indeed we might perhaps expect in a culture where the writer's own sister is called Soledad. Melquíades' chronicling of the story, and the subsequent deciphering of it, both depend on a willed seclusion. Writing is a homeopathic form of solitude which serves an ultimate purpose of solidarity. On this reading, the imaginary or vicarious nature of fiction has a positive purpose. Just as Cervantes' 'idle reader' learns of the disastrous effects of reading upon an idle man, so the nostalgia of the Buendías is nostalgically narrated.

And the same applies to solitude, the central motif of Márquez' *œuvre*. Artistic self-consciousness and the solitude theme are combined in Melquíades. He seems perhaps partly a trickster yet also a reminder of the lonely God of *In Evil Hour*. Whereas the divine Creator was necessarily lonely, Melquíades as a human being adopts his solitude for a creative purpose. On the one hand, he is the image of the writer as one whose meaning is incomprehensible until the reader has actually lived the experience. For there is no short-cut to wisdom through literature. But for anyone who wishes to take the trouble there are patterns and shapings to experience which literature can help us to understand. Most importantly, there are inner and emotional shapings which may be therapeutically re-enacted in the controlled seduction of fiction. That is why the reader needs to be in some measure seduced as well as aesthetically detached. To come to such fiction with a prior, ideological conviction of meaning, which the work can then only instantiate or otherwise, is likely to rob it of its proper working. It is an extraordinary achievement on Márquez' part to have combined this meditation on the enigma of literary meaning with such a weight of historical experience.

Melquíades embodies the deliberately enigmatic structure of the narrative by which it actively frustrates interpretative closure. Márquez' long-standing ambivalence about overtly 'political' writing, and his consequent meditation on the paradoxical relations of art and life, have resulted not just in a formal play with the fictitious historian but in an especially acute awareness of the necessary solitude which, if you can get it right, is really a profound form of solidarity.

5

The Magical and the Banal:
The Autumn of the Patriarch

The Autumn of the Patriarch is Márquez' distinctive contribution to a well recognised sub-genre of Latin American fiction: the 'dictator' novel.[1] The country in which it is set has a Caribbean coastline and an Andean hinterland but is otherwise unspecified, in accordance with Márquez' evident attempt to capture a more general regional myth rather than give a specific political analysis.

The novel opens with the discovery of the dictator's body already made unrecognisable by carrion birds in the run-down presidential palace. He has lived for over a hundred years and his story is unfolded in six long, sparsely punctuated flashbacks in which the narrative voices and the personal pronouns keep shifting without warning. The sense is clear enough but the everyday assumptions of identity in language are constantly disoriented. Each section opens with the initial moment of discovery to reveal some different aspect of the past. In this way Márquez is able repeatedly to spring narrative surprises reflecting the bottomless horror and deceptions of the dictatorship. A crucial event governing the present was the former occasion on which the death by poison of his secret double enabled the dictator to stage his own false death to test the loyalty of those around him. Even his rotting corpse is no sure indication of his death.

He is, with some reason, sexually insecure and his twin obsessions are sex and security. The only woman to whom he has ever completely exposed himself physically, including his huge herniated testicle, is the Indian girl, Leticia Nazareno, he has had removed from a convent to become his mistress. Her success with him is partly that she re-enacts his only true, if deeply retarded, human relationship which was with his mother. In the matter of security, he is equally caught in a regressive trap. Each of the figures he appoints to run his security system has, by the nature of the case, to become a danger to him. The more effective, the more dangerous.

It is evident that, as in *Hundred Years*, Márquez is giving the dictator theme a summative and mythopoeic treatment and once again he uses the blurring of reality and fantasy as his own narrative mode even while pointing it up as a symptomatic condition of the characters and situation. But the relation of character and theme to the narrative mode is different from in *Hundred Years* and in some respects more problematic in ways that have a bearing on larger shifts in narrative form over the latter part of Márquez' *œuvre*. The mode known as 'magical realism' is pushed to such an extreme in *Autumn* that it becomes almost an unconscious exorcism, or discovery of limits, for the mode itself.

I have already suggested that *Hundred Years* is a turning point in Márquez' work. The occasional and sub-textual concern of his earlier fiction with its own truth value became the thematic substance of *Hundred Years* as if a patterned fabric were to be reversed to reveal an even more subtle design on the other side. Hence its being both summative and atypical. To see *Hundred Years* in the light of this longer-term, implicit preoccupation helps in the understanding of *Autumn* and indeed much of the later fiction. For *Autumn* pre-dated *Hundred Years* in its conception, even though it was written after it, and *Autumn* therefore straddles the same period and to a significant extent complements *Hundred Years*. *Hundred Years* dealt with the twin themes of love and power under the sign of solitude and viewed this whole complex from the point of view of popular and private life. *Autumn* presents a comparable failure of love and sexuality through the 'vicio solitario del poder' / 'solitary vice of power' but it now attempts to address this theme within the very centre of political authority.[2] So too, the expansive, generous, Cervantean humour of *Hundred Years* contrasts with the taut, black humour of *Autumn*. We may recollect Márquez' early enthusiasm for Kafka, the eternal outsider, and find that the insider's view of the 'castle' is equally Kafkaesque.[3]

As with Kafka's novels and Beckett's plays, we soon recognise that the 'story', as a story, is not going to go anywhere. The interest rather lies in the intensified circling around a central focus which cannot itself be stated; or at least not without banality. Márquez' theme is less metaphysical but the comparable artistic challenge of his novel is to engage more directly with the 'banality of evil'; the difficult theme which was handled more obliquely in *In Evil Hour*. In that story, the personal vacuity of the mayor was vividly conveyed through its consequences for others. It resists handling more directly because there is nothing there to get hold of. That is part of the horror. But this is an artistic, as well as an ethical, problem and the more so as this ethical blank becomes the central focus of an extended work. What is effective as macabre humour in a short piece such as 'Big Mama's Funeral' is now raised to a new order of seriousness and scope.

In view of this fundamental artistic problem, one can understand why Márquez opted for a 'mythic' treatment and why, having done so, he went the whole hog and reached for a mode of sustained imaginative hyperbole. The book is full of memorable flights such as the dictator's selling the Caribbean Sea to pay off the national debt, or serving to his conspiring senior aides the roasted body of the would-be coup leader, General Rodrigo de Aguilar. This is not to say, of course, that the narrative is purely fanciful throughout. As with the massacre of the strikers in *Hundred Years*, historically realistic events are placed within a context of imaginative extremity as if this were their only possible company. *Autumn* intensifies this technique. Writing in the wake of the French Revolution, de Sade remarked that the gothic and sensational fiction of his day had been surpassed and put out of business by the horrors of history itself.[4] Much twentieth-century fiction has echoed this recognition and *Autumn* is as much a meditation on this imaginative quandary as it is a study of dictatorship, for the story in effect internalises the predicament as the dictator's own. He has survived by constantly out-bidding, keeping imaginatively ahead of, reality even as that reality includes the spiralling consequences of his own former extravagances. The polyphonic mixture of narrative voices enforces this sense of a large, uncontrollable process which he rides with the practised skill of a surf-rider always in danger of being engulfed if he does not keep a split second ahead. The barely punctuated prose enacts this unstoppable process in which he, as much as everyone else, is caught.

Yet *Autumn* has not proved to be one of Márquez' most popular books and the critical reception has been mixed. The imaginative world of the book has often excited respect rather than compelling involvement. Gerald Martin has criticised it in political terms. He sees it as insidiously perpetuating the myth of an old-style Latin American dictator.[5] On the face of it, he argues, the novel seems

properly severe and satirical but the archetype was already anachronistic at the time of writing. There may be something in that
objection although it does not sufficiently concede to the author the
right to work within his own premises and in that respect it echoes
the old criticism of Dickens that his supposedly reforming novels
were often written after the public consciousness on a particular
social question had already been aroused. But Dickens was usually
exploiting an existing popular consciousness of a social evil as a way
of developing a more universal and still relevant theme. The former
debtors' prison, the Marshalsea, was already destroyed at the time of
writing *Little Dorrit*, but the underlying evils of class snobbery and
money power were still rampant. The one theme is a Trojan horse for
penetrating the other and Márquez is clearly seeking to do something
similar.

Márquez' dictator, who has lived over a hundred years and
outlasted other living memory, is to be seen as a synoptic
historical myth. From his window the patriarch sees Columbus'
three caravels as well as the muddy bed of the sea now removed
to Arizona. As in *Hundred Years*, one implication may be to consign
all this to the past. In that respect it may be pointedly unrelated to
the immediate political present. But the overwhelming effect is to
establish a distance from any immediate history for a more universal
reflection on the illusions of power.

In a curious way, mythopoeic treatment *is* unhistorical yet can
constantly set up eerie and suggestive resonances even in the moving
historical present of a text's subsequent existence. Just as the suicide
and financial collapse of Robert Maxwell in 1992 echoed that of
Dickens' Merdle in *Little Dorrit*, so some of Márquez's details have
had subsequent echoes.[6] At a trivial level, the thousands of unworn
boots left by the ousted henchman Saenz de la Barra are like the
myriad shoes of Imelda Marcos on which the popular and journalistic
imagination focused when her husband's regime was ousted in the
Philippines.[7] More chillingly, the dictator's final method of ridding
himself of thousands of children who were witnesses to the brutality
of his regime was the use of cement-filled boats just outside territorial
waters. This was closely echoed in the apparent fate of many young
people, known as 'los desaparecidos', who disappeared in Argentina
in the 1970s. More significantly, perhaps, subsequent history suggests the relevance of such mythopoeic thought in understanding
historical events. Octavio Paz sought to account for the strange
collapse of the sophisticated military empire of the Aztecs to Cortez'

small invading force by explanations going beyond the military and political. He suggested that the Aztecs were a people who believed themselves deserted by their gods and suffering what he called 'imperial fatigue'.[8] The phrase may once have struck some readers as fanciful, too much of a poet's phrase, but the sudden collapse of the communist order in the USSR and its satellites at the end of the 1980s calls out for explanation at some such level. This is not to deny other levels of explanation for the sake of some mystical process, it is rather to see that the psychological whole is greater than, or different from, the sum of its externally definable parts. That is why there have to be occasional moments of grounding in ultimate values for all worldly institutions (such as law, politics or the military) whose successful day-to-day functioning depends on keeping a distance from them. These institutions are an inescapable necessity of modern life and it is part of the function of literature, although not its purpose, to affirm and understand ultimate values without being naïve or sentimental. Where this becomes too much the purpose, as great writers always recognised, the function suffers and the work becomes merely one-dimensional. As I have repeatedly observed, this complex relation of the literary and the journalistic has been a constant preoccupation of Márquez' career; in *Autumn* he has moved to one end of the spectrum to create a summative expression of the hollowness of political power when conceived as an end in itself. It is perhaps rare in life that the power motive is *consciously* conceived in this way, it is usually attached to a conviction of public interest, and Márquez' novel is an attempt to meditate on the illusory structure of power in a way that the complexities of any real-life situation will almost inevitably obscure.

In short, Márquez has to be granted his mythopoeic premises and if there is indeed a reservation about *Autumn* it needs to be understood in more intrinsic terms. The same applies to the different objection raised by Philip Swanson, who sees the figure of the patriarch as too sympathetically presented.[9] Once again, an intelligent and responsive critic offers what is surely an extrinsic criterion to explain a dissatisfaction which must have a more intrinsic cause. Authors can do anything they want provided they make it work. It is the artistic failure, if it is such, that has to be understood. Swanson's point, although he may be right in the event, actually suggests the positive effect at which Márquez was evidently aiming. Márquez clearly needs his dictator to be human. However marginally, he is to be recognisably 'one of us'.[10] The mayor of *In Evil Hour* was given toothache to establish a basis of common humanity and there are similar touches with the patriarch such as his hernia, his tinnitus, his severe headaches and above all the universal experience of ageing.

Marquez is seeking to broaden his theme and needs to deflect the standard responses to such a figure. In this connection, his own suggestion of an autobiographical stake in the book needs to be taken seriously. For by the time of writing the novel Márquez had become a public figure and he has remarked on the impact of this experience on the novel.[11] He now saw how, apart from its obvious advantages, fame also restricted him and changed the nature of his personal relationships. Particularly with new acquaintances, and even with older ones, a question would now hang over their motives and conduct in relation to him. Ironically, it was a work of fiction which had changed his life and part of the change was that his very fame had introduced a fictive dimension into his own life. Márquez had discovered radical distrust without needing to be evil. As well as the necessary and natural solitude of the creative writer, he now encountered the enforced solitude of fame which is experienced in the crowd. All this suggests why the political theme of the dictator is assimilated to a more morally neutral and metaphysical concern.

If the situation of the dictator has some analogy with that of the writer of fiction this may be partly summed up as an especially problematic relationship to others. Something of this may be seen in the episode in which the dictator's Indian mistress and his young son are torn to pieces by specially trained fighting dogs.

> ... dos de sus edecanes irrumpieron en la oficina con la novedad terrible de que a Leticia Nazareno y al niño los habían descuartizado y se los habían comido a pedazos los perros cimarrones del mercado público, se los comieron vivos mi general, pero no eran los mismos perros callejeros de siempre sino unos animales de presa con unos ojos amarillos atónitos y una piel lisa de tiburón que alguien había cebado contra los zorros azules, sesenta perros iguales que nadie supo cuándo saltaron de entre los mesones de legumbres y cayeron encima de Leticia Nazareno y el niño sin darnos tiempo de disparar por miedo de matarlos a ellos que parecía como si estuvieran ahogándose junto con los perros en un torbellino de infierno, sólo veíamos los celajes instantáneos de unas manos efímeras tendidas hacia nosotros mientras el resto del cuerpo iba desapareciendo a pedazos, veíamos unas expresiones fugaces y inasibles que a veces

eran de terror, a veces eran de lástima, a veces de júbilo, hasta que
acabaron de hundirse en el remolino de la rabatiña y sólo quedó
flotando el sombrero de violetas de fieltro de Leticia Nazareno
ante el horror impasible de las verduleras totémicas salpicadas de
sangre . . . (p. 254)

. . . two of his aides burst into his office with the terrible news
that Leticia Nazareno and the child had been torn apart and
eaten piece by piece by the stray dogs in the public market,
they ate them alive general, but they weren't the same street
dogs as usual but hunting animals with yellow, astonished eyes
and smooth skins like sharks that someone had set upon the
blue foxes, sixty dogs all alike who nobody knew when they
leaped out from between the vegetable stalls and fell on top of
Leticia Nazareno and the child without giving us time to shoot for
fear of killing them who looked as if they were drowning beside
the dogs in a hellish vortex, we could see only the momentary
tokens of ephemeral hands reaching towards us while the rest
of the body was disappearing in pieces, we saw fleeting and
ungraspable expressions that were sometimes of terror, at other
times of pity, at other times of jubilation until they finally sank
into the whirlpool of the scramble and there remained only Leticia
Nazareno's hat with felt violets floating in front of the impassive
horror of the totemic vegetable women spattered with blood . . .
(p. 152)

This horrific event is recounted with a filmic detachment which
is itself worth pausing on. Narration is a form of relation and
how can one either relate, or relate to, such events? Ever since
the fiction of moral sentiment in the eighteenth century, astute
authors have been aware of the moral quagmire on which fictional
occasions seeking to arouse strong emotional response actually rest.
Voyeurism, pornography and complacency lurk constantly beneath
such attempts, even the best intentioned, since fictional events
must always command a different response from real ones and the
emotions aroused by extreme situations are difficult to contain artistically. The downward shift in the meaning of the terms 'sentimental'
and 'complacency' since the cult of sentiment is an index of the care
with which self-serving sentimentality, in the modern sense, has now
to be avoided.[12] Márquez has found a way of building the problem
into the narrative so that the horror of the episode is communicated

without his needing to adopt any authorial posture which might implicitly appropriate it.

The novel allows no single narrative voice to stand over and against the events but creates rather a polyphony of nervously interested voices constantly emerging from, and fading back into, the action they collectively recount. In the present episode, Márquez' initial invocation of the guards' own voices highlights the modulation into a more impersonal narrative voice as the incident moves to its climax. At the central moment, the prose, along with the extended image of it all taking place in water, slows the whole action down. It is like one of those moments of filmic violence, such as in *Bonnie and Clyde* (1967), where the camera goes literally into slow motion. At such moments it may be a delicate matter to distinguish an overt aesthetic control of difficult material from a voyeuristic lingering. Here it is clearly the former and partly because this problematic is at the heart of the narrative throughout. In using the guards at this point as narrators assimilated to his own narrative voice, Márquez negotiates this problem and is even perhaps implicitly thematising it as a problem. The ancient device of the messenger, familiar from Greek tragedy, becomes a way not of keeping the horror off-stage but of bringing into focus the difficulty of telling such things at all. In a narrative, after all, there is no need to report things as 'offstage' unless the act of reporting is significant in itself.

In the present instance, this effect of authorial disappearance is reinforced by the fact that, although we are given no specific reason to distrust the guards' account, the general impact of the narrative is to suggest that no one is trustworthy and, for all we know, the guards may themselves have been implicated in the plot. Is the guards' narration one of genuine horror at the event; or secret satisfaction at it; or is fear of its consequences for themselves leading them to pile it on? In so far as these questions are implicit in the narrative they focus the whole question of what narrative, or human, relation can be adopted towards such events. This uncertainty as to whether the guards were indeed horrified and helpless, or were refusing to intervene, helps to give a Flaubertian detachment to the episode without allowing this to become an authorial posture. Flaubert wished the impersonality to be felt as an active expression of the artist's vision. In Márquez, the effect is felt to arise from the situation while recognising that the observer or narrator is an indissoluble aspect of the event. Any event which is humanly known at all is, inescapably, an object of human 'relation'.

Fictional 'relation' is always double-edged. It may be a means of emotional insight into others or it may be a way of seeing the other as a fiction. This latter possibility echoes the extreme psychotic condition seen in mass-murderers, torturers and tyrants. *Autumn* is a book which studies, and enacts, this sinister underside of fiction as a model of de-realisation. For what the narrative communicates throughout is not so much the 'unreliability' of the narrators in the conventional sense so much as their consciousness of the pervasive unreliability of their world. The polyphony of narrative voices in *Autumn* creates a mutual play of mirror images in which everything you see may be illusory. This is the potentially metaphysical inflection of the dictator theme. From its very opening sentence, *Hundred Years* had joked with its own narrative unreliability but in *Autumn* unreliability is a more grimly humorous matter.

Given Márquez' long-standing meditation on the nature of fiction, the theme of the dictator was perhaps inevitably to acquire for him a strongly metaphysical, rather than a simply political, inflection. At the core of the story we can imagine Borges' unwritten version of it: the dictator who has had to set up a series of deceptive fictions for others is himself inevitably trapped, is indeed the most trapped, within their spiralling logic of universal distrust. Márquez presents his dictator as trapped within such a Borgesian labyrinth of virtuality. Appropriately, the patriarch's moment of nostalgic envy of 'real' power occurs in the theatre although he, of course, is incapable of the Borgesian metaphysical insight the experience might have afforded him.

As it happens, the artist in question here is the great modern Nicaraguan poet, Rubén Darío(1867–1916). Darío is a leitmotif of the novel and Márquez is perhaps insinuating that although the dictator figure is one of the great myths of Latin America, the region could just as well be known for its imaginative energy and verve. And indeed the work of Márquez' own generation has done much to effect precisely that change in perception. The patriarch's envious recognition ' . . . eso sí es un desfile, no las mierdas que me organiza esta gente . . . ' (p. 248) / ' . . . this really is a parade, not the crap these people organise for me . . . ' (p. 148) hints at the two men being different inflections of a common cultural possibility. And for the reader, of course, there is the deeper contrast that the patriarch, apart from his personal vacuity, is ostentatiously a fictional being, a product of words, while Darío's splendour of language is an historical fact. Darío's reality caps the patriarch's tawdry fiction.

It is also significant that, despite the pointedly theatrical setting of the episode, Márquez has chosen in Darío not an actor, playwright, or other artist of fictional illusion, but a poet. The poet's medium is more directly the language itself. Maybe, in this world of bottomless deception, it is true, as Yeats said, that 'words alone are certain good'.[13] And seen in this light, Márquez' novel seems to place itself between Darío and the patriarch. Márquez is not Darío, but the brutal fantasies of the patriarch, which make up the substance of the narrative, are mediated through an unashamedly poetic prose. As in the passage just quoted, the most brutal events require an equivalent intensity of meditation rather than the literal intensity of apparently direct witness. It is as if on the literalistic plane there can be no adequate response. Direct witness cauterises into silence and the rest is literature. Theodore Adorno's famous remark that there can be no poetry after Auschwitz becomes a piece of well-meaning pretentiousness when it circulates as a free-floating generalisation. One might rather say that Auschwitz makes poetry more necessary. But it undoubtedly points to an important ethical and artistic problem felt with special urgency in the latter half of the twentieth century. Márquez, in effect, takes the strong line in recognising that only literature can contemplate these things and he brings to bear an ostentatious verbal density as the means to hold horrors in contemplative focus. Undoubtedly, this approach too has its dangers and the book seems to me on the whole a triumph of tact in never merely converting horror into poetry. Poetry is its means of discipline. In this respect, the poetry of the book's medium is more crucial than the fact that this is his most 'magically' hyperbolic novel at the level of narrative content.

The ostentatiously poetic density of the narrative language also suggests how Márquez' metaphysical theme does not necessarily slight the political one. For an implicit, silent scream is the constant underside of the novel's enjoyment of its own baroque articulacy. In this respect, it is instructive to compare the novel with some comparably metaphysical works in which the issue of violence is not so addressed or felt. At one level, Márquez' novel echoes one of the most famous works of the Spanish baroque, Calderon's *Life is a Dream* (1636), in which the young prince becomes a good and effective king, at least in contemporary terms, after acquiring metaphysical insight into the illusory nature of power, and goes on to show a corresponding capacity to exercise it, when necessary, with surgical speed and detachment. But from a modern viewpoint the monarchical ethic of the play is uncomfortably close to the standpoint of Márquez' patriarch and, indeed, Calderon's play embodies some part of the ancestry of tyrannical leadership in the modern Hispanic world. Meanwhile, on the other side of the political spectrum, Jean Genet's *The Balcony* (1956), which uses the brothel as a house of illusion, encompasses the political domain within its essentially metaphysical action but real political consequences remain notional in Genet just as they would do in the elegant version of the theme we might imagine Borges to have written. For Genet, any actual violence is an algebraical 'x' in the metaphysical equation whereas Márquez, by contrast, stresses at all times the real horror within the play of illusion and, just as importantly, he brings out the inextricably causal relation between them. In a world where nothing is certain there can be no half-measures. As Machiavelli made clear, anyone who is to be destroyed must be destroyed immediately, absolutely, and often in an exemplary manner.

Violence is, therefore, a function of illusion in this story in a way that gives it a structural logic. Illusion arises from, and feeds, insecurity, which in turn deepens the sense of unreality. And by the same logic, the patriarch's psychotic, retarded incapacity to imagine the 'otherness' of his fellow beings infects the reality of the world for them too. In that respect the patriarch is a negative Quixote. Like Quixote, he has created a would-be heroic fiction and draws others, for a variety of motives, into participating in it. But he is negative in a more radical sense than in substituting his evil for Quixote's altruism. He is a centre of negative being, a black hole into which a necessary confidence in the reality of a shared world is sucked and lost. Whereas Quixote's illusions ultimately enhance the sense of reality in the book in which he appears, the patriarch drains his world of reality. And, not incidentally, he thereby destroys the consensual world on which the realist novel depends.[14]

Another way of putting the point, therefore, is to say that the patriarch is himself a kind of magical realist in so far as this imaginative mode has been defined, in contrast to fantasy, as one in which the distinction between 'reality' and 'fantasy' is elided.[15] He has created a world in which he can no longer tell where fantasy stops and reality starts, and he imposes this uncertainty on others. For him, of course, this is not a fictional technique but a confused condition. Yet maybe the book is itself in some measure drawn into this condition. Whereas in *Hundred Years* there was a humorous gap between the Buendias' obsessions and the magical mode of the narrative, in

Autumn the book itself struggles with the condition it describes. To see the patriarch as a magical realist, albeit in bad faith and *malgré lui*, is a more intrinsic way of explaining the readerly and critical resistance the book has aroused.

The narrative method of constantly shifting voices linked in a continuous unparagraphed flow with few full stops aptly expresses the claustrophobia and unstoppability of the process in which the characters are trapped. But it seems artistically claustrophobic too. It is as if the 'banality of evil' as embodied in the patriarch is a black hole into which the imaginative energy and resourcefulness of the writing has to be infinitely hurled without ever filling the space. The occasional, overt technique of wholesale repetition of the patriarch's final posture in death seems almost to figure forth this creative frustration. For once, Márquez' narrative technique is visible on the surface as if emphasising his bitter circling around an empty centre.

The crux of the artistic problem may be focused by contrast with Shakespeare's dramatic cunning in handling the tyrant theme in *Macbeth*. All the historical evidence seems to be that the figures who have perpetrated political terror do not have the quality of remorse which most people would have if they had such deeds on their conscience. That is partly why they have been able to do these things. There are, of course, many interesting mixed cases in fiction, such as Dostoevsky's Raskolnikov, and in real life, such as the reformed ex-torturers of former regimes. It is possible for remorse to come later. But such figures seem if anything to confirm the general point. In the imaginative context of a poetic, tragic drama Shakespeare is able to splice together two necessary, but incompatible, aspects of his central figure in such a way that we do not notice the join. Shakespeare's tragic conception needed evil ambition and remorse simultaneously within the same consciousness. Partly by splitting the theme between Macbeth and Lady Macbeth, he is able to present in Macbeth a realistically unlikely combination of evil and remorse.

But Márquez' purposes are, of course, very different from Shakespeare's in his different historical circumstances. In our secularised culture, and with our more general recognition of the problem of banality as identified by Arendt, it is less appropriate to project a moral consciousness into such a figure and harder to place a telling metaphysic around him. The *Macbeth* solution was no longer available to Márquez as it was still to Dostoevsky.

The horrors of twentieth-century history have, we might say, left two artistic blank spots; areas which seem to resist adequate treatment while constantly calling out for it. These are the experiences of the victims and the inner condition of the perpetrators. Márquez attempts both in this book. If there is a sense of staring into the sun, of attempting to articulate the ineffable, this seems to lie in the nature of the case and is in some measure recognised in the style of closely disciplined yet straining hyperbole in which the book is written. If the book can get no closer to the reality it yet seems to maintain an honourable consciousness of its own limitation.

Where so many of history's real-life victims, who are generically invoked in the book, can do no more than scratch their names on cell walls, the writer of this fiction at least allows himself no easy cooption of their suffering. If the book is more difficult to read than some, this is perhaps in part because Márquez intuitively resists any easy ride on the historical power of the theme. What I take from the responses of both Martin and Swanson is that the sheer horror of the story leads the reader inevitably and properly to think of the living history beyond the text. But this in itself closes the creative circle. If the horrors within the fiction are only justified by our thinking of the real ones for which they stand, then this very thought makes literary treatment seem an impertinence. The poetic density of this text seems to arise from the effort to keep the emotional power of the material within the imaginative frame of the book. And the non-realistic mode makes it peculiarly necessary to do this, which would not be the case in a frankly documentary narrative.

Reflection on the difficult artistic project of *Autumn* suggests why the fiction/life relation is still an active concern for Márquez in this book albeit in slightly different way. The journalism/fiction theme is incidentally thematised in the patriarch's studying the graffiti in the toilets to get his news while special editions of the newspaper and of the soap-opera are produced just for him. This suggests a change in emphasis which extends into Márquez' later career. After a number of political novellas, all sharing a latent or subtextual concern with the truth claims of fiction, *Hundred Years* brought this concern to the surface through the Cervantean device of an 'historical' narrative nested within an overtly magical fiction. In the novels that immediately follow *Hundred Years* we tend rather to find characters living out their respective, mischievous fictions within an historical world.

But the patriarch is an extreme case. He is trapped, and to some extent traps us too, in the spiralling logic of his magical realism.

Whereas Márquez' distinctive ability lies in his apparently casual, hidden artistry, the creative logic of his conception here requires a sustained *tour de force*; a constantly heightened pitch from which it is difficult not to flinch. If Shakespeare could successfully engage a related problem this was primarily because of a difference in historical and philosophical circumstances, but it is also relevant that he was a poetic dramatist and in fact all the ready analogies drawn in this chapter have been from theatre. This suggests that the question of genre may be an important way of addressing broader questions of fictional meaning. In his next novella, Márquez was in fact to move away from the mode of magical realism and actively exploit the different framings of experience offered respectively by tragedy and novel.

6

Male Tragedy/Female Novella: *Chronicle of a Death Foretold*

Márquez once identified his next novella as his most satisfactory artistic achievement.[1] I share this view while continuing to find *No One Writes* more perfect and *Hundred Years* more ambitious and substantial. Like *Hundred Years*, *Chronicle* has an enigma at its core but it is constructed and narrated, despite its apparent casualness, with a limpid clarity and close logic.

Once again the original germ of the story goes back to an incident in Márquez' early life which he had long wished to treat in a fiction. When a young bride, Angela Vicario, in a small Colombian town, is found by her new husband, Bayardo San Román, not to be a virgin, he returns her to her strict religious family. Under pressure to reveal the name of her seducer she names the narrator's friend, Santiago Nasar, although it is never clear whether he is indeed the culprit and, if not, why exactly she should name him. But her twin brothers now feel themselves to be under an obligation of honour to kill Santiago and thereby restore her good name. They prepare for the killing with such openness that their preparations are taken by many as mere bravado, with the result that, despite the eventual knowledge of almost the whole town, Santiago is not warned until too late and is publicly butchered in the main square. The narrator returns some twenty years later and the story consists of his attempt to piece together the crucial hours and to understand why the so evidently impending catastrophe was not averted.

The lucidly logical concentration of this novella is in sharp contrast to the wide-ranging historical and mythopoeic ambition of *Hundred Years*. But there may be a closer relationship between these two different achievements; the later one being partly made possible by the earlier. For *Chronicle*, in a different way again from *Autumn*, also reverses many of the terms of *Hundred Years*. Most crucially, it inverts the formal relation of 'history' and 'fiction'. If it were taken in isolation, the title of *Chronicle of a Death Foretold* could more readily suggest the standpoint of Melquíades' prophetic chronicle enfolded within Márquez' earlier novel. In the later novel, by contrast, the term 'chronicle' refers to the narrator's own historical account which constitutes the actual text of the novella. In the earlier book, that is to say, both the history and the fictitious historian are placed within the larger frame of the fiction. In the later work, the historical enquiry constitutes the ultimate frame of the fiction and this effect is reinforced by the fact that the narrator is himself using as a partial source the earlier enquiry of a previous judicial investigator.

The mutually reinforcing impact of these two enquiries becomes particularly evident in the last section as we gradually withdraw from the suspense of the main action to replace it once again within the enigmatic fixture of its historical frame. The actual complexity of this, along with the typically limpid naturalness, can be seen in a passage such as the following where the narrator comments on the surviving pages of the earlier investigator's report:

> El nombre del juez no apareció en ninguno, pero es evidente que era un hombre abrasado por la fiebre de la literatura. Sin duda había leído a los clásicos españoles, y algunos latinos, y conocía muy bien a Nietzsche, que era el autor de moda entre los magistrados de su tiempo. Las notas marginales, y no sólo por el color de la tinta, parecían escritas con sangre. Estaba tan perplejo con el enigma que le había tocado el suerte, que muchas veces incurrio en distracciones líricas contrarias al rigor de su oficio. Sobre todo, nunca le pareció legítimo que la vida se serviera de tantas casualidades prohibidas a la literatura, para que se cumpliera sin tropiezos una muerte tan anunciada.[2]

> The judge's name did not appear on any of them, but he was obviously a man burning with the fever of literature. He had undoubtedly read the Spanish classics, and a few Latin ones, and had a good knowledge of Nietzsche who was the fashionable author among magistrates of his time. The marginal notes, and

not just because of the colour of the ink, seemed written in blood. He was so perplexed by the enigma that chance had dealt him that he fell over and again into lyrical digressions quite against the rigour of his professional office. Above all, it never seemed legitimate to him that life should make use of so many coincidences forbidden to literature so as to fulfil without hindrance a death so amply foretold.[3]

Just like Cervantes' narrative intermediaries, the judge cannot refrain from intruding his own comments. But his effect is to reinforce, rather than to undermine or fictionalise, the 'historical' frame of the narrative. He also points up the embarrassment of the present narrator as he too stares into the same history to find over and again the features of fiction. And by the same token, this narrator, who is not such a literary man, highlights the more acute sense of this predicament in the investigating judge who partakes overtly of the same vertiginous anxiety that we have seen to be constantly running just beneath the surface of all Márquez' fiction. It is the anxiety of a man with a powerful sense of the claims of both literary and of historical truth but who finds them, as if for that very reason, perpetually dissolving into each other. As Thomas Mann was aware, when he found his own contemplation of contemporary history dissolving increasingly into myth, a diet of the Spanish classics topped up and modernised by Nietzsche would do much to intensify, and to raise the metaphysical stakes, of this predicament.[4]

Of course, the immediate impact of the double frame here is lightly to ironise these Marquesian preoccupations of the judge but the more substantial underlying effect is to make us aware of this metaphysical dimension pervading the narrative consciousness at large and touching the heart of the subject-matter. Indeed, as the present paragraph makes its sinuous way to the dying fall of the title clause it casually gathers in the pure 'chance' of the judge's being involved in the case at all before finally commenting on the unacceptable degree of literary coincidence in the historical events. The term coincidence, which seems a necessary yardstick in both legal and literary critical contexts, starts to dissolve before our eyes.

These categories are invoked in the abstract so as to be dissolved in reality. *Hundred Years* took a Cervantean delight in its narrative equivocations but *Chronicle*, as the use of the deliberately humble term 'chronicle' rather than 'history' implies, seeks to eschew such narrative duplicities only to demonstrate the more forcefully the intractable uncertainties of the events themselves. Thus the very opening sentence of *Hundred Years* deliberately misleads the reader with its implication that Col. Aureliano is to die before a firing squad. By contrast, the opening of *Chronicle*, 'El día en que lo iban a matar, Santiago Nasar...' (p. 9) / 'On the day he was to be killed, Santiago Nasar...' (p. 1), gives us the plain fact. There is a similar difference of spirit in the fact that José Arcadio kills out of a sense of wounded honour but also impetuous anger when Prudencio Aquilar imprudently provokes him. Santiago, on the other hand, is seen at the beginning of *Chronicle* exercising an exemplary prudence, if not in the sexual sphere which is to be his downfall, then at least in keeping his gun and bullets in different parts of the house. Not only is the historical quest of the narrator carried out in a spirit of sober earnest, the narrative which he unfolds is ostentatiously prosaic in its content and texture.

This constant blurring of fiction and history is experienced in an even more complex way by the reader than it is by the narrator of the story. For the reader is aware of the whole narrative as fictional and that in turn gives a special edge to much of the action in which imaginative projections akin to fiction provide one of the psychological mainsprings.

The very name of the Vicario family hints at this. In general terms it is clear that their present fortune is below their remembered status and this explains their peculiar commitment to living up to a code. But their name suggests a fundamental posture of acting vicariously for some principle beyond themselves rather than from personal motive. It has been shrewdly suggested that if, as seems to be hinted, Angela was not in fact seduced by Santiago, then she was perhaps vicariously assuming this role on behalf of all the other young girls he had seduced or forced but whose honour was not going to be so assiduously defended.[5] The very fact that she should think of him in this connection, even if only at a venture, suggests some such deeper logic to her choice.

More importantly, the Vicario brothers are living up to a principle which they do not wish, and partly know they do not wish, to carry out. They deliberately overact their parts. The half-conscious motive of the brothers' ostentatious preparations is that they wish someone to stop them so that the point of honour will have been satisfied by their manifest intention without their needing to kill

Santiago with whom they have been celebrating only the previous night.

The publicly demonstrated intention combined with a forcible restraint would have provided a necessary fiction and saved them from the need for its literal enactment. But by an irony which has an irrefragable logic and psychological truth, their very ostentatiousness prevents people taking them seriously. The outcome for the Vicarios is that other people do indeed detect the element of fiction in their behaviour but misinterpret its point. And, of course, it is an important part of the overall logic that the brothers are by no means so clear in their own minds about this distinction as such an analytic summary may make it appear. For if the brothers were indeed more clear about this secret motive then their sense of honour would no longer be satisfied. Both the intention and the restraint would have to be real for them, just as they were for Don Quixote when he was defeated and sent back home by Sanson Carrasco disguised as the 'Knight of the Moon'.[6] They would have to be both physically overcome and persuaded that their return home was according to the requirements of their code of honour. It is worth remarking that in Cervantes quixotic behaviour is usually male with women being the sane or saving figures. This is clearly the case in Márquez' tale and it is interesting that the characters named Miguel and Cervantes are both female.

The mixed mental state of the Vicario brothers is partly reminiscent of the Buendías. The brothers are described before the killing as being like 'sonámbulos desvelados' (p. 25) / 'insomniac sleepwalkers' (p. 14) and the point is highlighted by their afterwards feeling, in Pablo's own words, as if they were 'despierto dos veces' (p. 103) / 'awake twice over' (p. 100). Perhaps part of Márquez' apparent unease with *Hundred Years* was that its great popular success had almost certainly been contingent on a sentimentalised reading. The 'magical realism' arising from his strategic use of the dream consciousness of his characters can lead readers to participate in the sympathetic 'magic' at the expense of the critical 'realism' of the book.

Hence, although Márquez has always maintained a proper reserve with respect to any such direct critique of *Hundred Years*, *Chronicle* effectively constitutes a more astringent, and partly inverted, reworking of its structure and themes. The code of the Vicarios is clearly unhealthy and anachronistic; the pervasive *machismo* of the culture is seen in a consistently sardonic way; and the equivocations of history and fiction are a matter of anxiety to the narrator himself who has the soberness of a responsible journalist. In this respect, a larger shape begins to emerge in the *œuvre*. The narrative equivocation with the believable in *Hundred Years* was followed by the Patriarch's creation of a magical realist confusion in *Autumn*. Both are now followed by a realist analysis of fictive postures and states of belief in *Chronicle*.

All this is not to say that *Chronicle* implies some rejection of these previous works. Each has its own inner logic which includes the later recognitions. But there is nonetheless a tension between these distinct imaginative worlds which enables us to perceive each one differently when we see them collectively. When Yeats put his poems into a deliberate *œuvre* this included as part of its meaning a sense that individual poems qualified, as well as enriched, each other. If Márquez has some reservation about *Hundred Years* it should be understood in the same spirit. What is at stake is not some intrinsic 'weakness' of that work so much as a desire, perhaps partly unconscious, to relativise it within the overall meaning of the *œuvre*.

The astringent impact of *Chronicle* within the *œuvre* therefore is not manifest in a direct, critical revisiting of earlier works so much as in a fresh vision of the nature of such 'fictional' or 'literary' models of behaviour in the lives of the characters. The Vicario brothers provide the obvious mainspring of the action through an anachronistic code of honour which leads them to become trapped within their own fiction. But the epigraph is taken from a short poem by the Portuguese poet Gil Vicente (1465?–1537) which invokes an anachronistic note with respect to the whole work and particularly in relation to Santiago Nasar. The poem warns the falcon (grammatically male) of the danger it courts in attacking a heron (female). Santiago, of course, practises the sport of hawking. In a way this suggests that this side of his character, unlike the hunting of him by the Vicarios, is securely contained within the convention of a sport. This is in keeping with his prudent handling of his weapons. But in his relations with women he enacts the mores of hawking in real life and, of course, his initial prophetic dream is of being soiled by the liquid droppings of birds. In that part of the world, a common way of catching birds is by throwing water over them and in death Santiago is like 'un pajarito mojado' (p. 149) / 'a little wet bird' (p. 116).

This invocation of anachronistic male values affects the story in several ways and at different narrative levels. At an immediate dramatic level it is necessary to see Santiago as innocent, for all we know, of the offence for which he is killed, although at the same time he must not become merely an object of sentimentally innocent pathos. His treatment of women, as fed through the image of falconry, gives him a significant personal failing while enabling us to understand this in terms of his own anachronistic code. He simply does not see the question in the way that most of his modern readers presumably do. Meanwhile the invocation of this code gives a more impersonal edge to the whole situation and makes him an intrinsic part of the larger logic by which the Vicarios feel obliged to become his killers. At the level of personal and social psychology, therefore, the epigraph gives an antique gem-like brilliance to the anachronistic and confused behaviour of many of the central characters. It allows us to understand, if not to approve, the poetic gleam which for some of them lies behind the prosaic surface of their lives.

Yet the epigraph, as well as bearing directly on Santiago, introduces the story as a whole. And this alerts us to the Flaubertian double irony of the narrative whereby a poetic gleam comes off the highly polished prose of the narrative in contrast to the sordid prosaicism of the life described. In that respect, this is Márquez' most Flaubertian work although it is still quite distinct in spirit from Flaubert's aestheticism. In Márquez' case, the artistic self-consciousness has a more actively thematic function within the work. Indeed, the problem of the novella's meaning is closely bound up with the question of where exactly we locate its poetry and its prose.

For poetry and prose suggest different ways of perceiving and valuing the 'same' experience. When the Canon of Toledo told Don Quixote that the 'epic may be written in prose as well as verse' their own author, Cervantes, was at that very moment showing the enormous consequences of doing so: he was creating the novel form.[7] The conscious recourse to Cervantes by several modern Latin American writers is to recover something of his nostalgic interplay of the marvellous, or the poetic, with the everyday. In this body of writing these elements tend to be given a more equal, if incommensurable, value. Borges' essay 'Partial Magic in the *Quixote*' at once argues and itself exemplifies this.[8] In the present work, a conflict between poetic and prosaic vision reflects the absoluteness of a traditional code of honour as against the complex, uncertain, mundane world of the action. It also reflects the conflict between the narrator's desire to understand the precise process leading to Santiago's death and the aura of tragic fatalism which has come to surround that death and by which it was perhaps partly caused. Yet, as in *Hundred Years*, while clearly critical of such honour and such fatalism, the story also recognises, in a thoroughly inward way, their power as human motives.

Indeed, some of the blurb on the cover of the standard English translation of *Chronicle* would suggest that the fatalistic sentiments to be found within the book have been seen as expressing the ultimate vision of the work itself. This is a suggestive misreading. It seems likely that *Hundred Years* had lent itself to such a fatalistic interpretation and that led in turn to *Chronicle* being perceived in the same light. But if *Chronicle* indeed echoes this theme of *Hundred Years*, it is only in order to challenge the more clearly such a fatalistic interpretation. Yet at the same time it must be said that both works do encompass dramatically the brooding emotional power of a fatalistic vision. Hence, in *Chronicle*, novelistic critique is combined with a sense of tragic enigma. Or in more immediately practical terms, the work examines the central events through the twin lenses of journalistic investigation and the structure of tragedy.

This doubleness can be seen in the ambiguous use of the word 'tragedy' throughout. When, for example, Clotilde Armenta ' . . . gritó a Cristo Bedoya que se diera prisa, porque en este pueblo de maricas sólo un hombre como el' podía impedir la tragedia' (p. 142) / ' . . . shouted to Cristo Bedoya to hurry up, because in that town full of faggots only a man like him could stop the tragedy' (p. 110) the word sits somewhere between the journalistic usage, as referring to a painful event of some magnitude, and the literary usage which is part of a metaphysical vision and, as Joyce's Stephen puts it, unites the human suffering with its 'secret cause'.[9] But these polar possibilities are felt to lurk in this casual usage only because they are actively highlighted and differentiated in the twin lenses of the narrative at large. As, for example, in the following passage:

> Para la inmensa mayoría sólo hubo una víctima: Bayardo San Román. Suponían que los otros protagonistas de la tragedia habían cumplido con dignidad, y hasta con cierta grandeza, la parte de favor que la vida les tenía señalada. (p. 109)

For the great majority there was only one victim: Bayardo San Román. They assumed that the other protagonists in the tragedy had been fulfilling with dignity, and even with a certain nobility, their part in the fortune that life had allotted to them. (p. 84)

The idea of tragedy is introduced here as an inextricable element in the collective psychology of the town. The events cannot be understood without it. But of course even in this last usage the term is not purely literary: the townspeople fail to distinguish the two domains and this failure lies at the heart of the action. By the same token, Márquez' artistic cunning and psychological lucidity lie in his own enfolding of this perceived 'tragedy' within the realist world of his novella:

This double frame of fatalistic tragedy and critical realism is artistically right because it is appropriate to the peculiarly public nature of the emotional life within the given culture. It is not just the specific question of honour which privileges public appearance over personal feeling. The essential sensibility is more widespread. The same spirit can be seen, for example, in the narrator's comment on the extravagant grief of Bayardo's family as they come to remove him, almost dying, from the town:

Antes de pisar tierra firme se quitaron los zapatos y atravesaron las calles hasta la colina caminando decalzas en el polvo ardiente del medio día, arrancándose mechones de raíz y llorando con gritos tan desgarradores que parecían de júbilo. Yo las vi pasar desde el balcón de Magdalena Oliver, y recuerdo haber pensado que un desconsuelo como ese sólo podía fingirse para ocultar otras vergüenzas mayores. (pp. 111–12)

Before stepping onto the ground, they took off their shoes and then went barefoot through the streets towards the hill in the burning midday dust, tearing out locks of hair by the roots and weeping with such piercing cries that they seemed to be from joy. I watched them pass from Magdalena Oliver's balcony and I remember thinking that anguish like that could only be assumed to cover up other and greater shames. (p. 86)

Such overt displays of grief have a cathartic value increasingly lost in modern Westernised culture. But the display may also have unconscious meanings as the narrator obscurely intuits. It is obscure because the full meaning of such a manifestation of grief may not be clear even to the individuals concerned, let alone to an observer. As with the Vicario brothers, there may be aspects to the public display which are not, indeed cannot, be recognised by the participants. In a curious way, it is precisely the most public dimension of such behaviour that may be the most unconscious. The display subsumes and covers up the private feelings. Just as the Buendías' unconscious structures were projected onto the 'real world' of *Hundred Years*, so in *Chronicle* there exists an anachronistic but historically real culture in which to sustain a comparably twilight zone of consciousness. In the present case, for example, the note of joy suggested by the narrator picks up what may be a satisfaction in the performance of grief and also the Dionysiac pleasure of abandoning the self to participate in a collective emotion. Yet such a recognition in no way impugns the authenticity of the grief. As usual, the narrator, watching from a balcony, embodies Márquez' sense of being both inside and outside the culture at the same time.

If we think of this display of grief in literary rather than anthropological terms, its classic ancestor is Don Quixote's conscious imitation of Beltenebros' penance.[10] Except that the terms are now reversed. Whereas we knew what Cervantes' hero was up to, Márquez' narrator looks from the balcony at a performance whose meaning is not fully open either to him or to us. Márquez' double framing of his story so that a would-be heroic code is set in critical yet transformative interaction with the everyday world is as crucial to this novella as it was, more obviously, to Cervantes. Although Márquez came at the end of the realist adventure which Cervantes did so much to initiate, and he has therefore inherited a different set of generic possibilities and tensions, he shares with Cervantes the sense that large, partly unconscious, cultural structures are embodied within literary genres themselves.

In Márquez' century, for example, it has been a much mooted question whether there can be a truly modern, post-nihilist tragedy or whether some kind of residually religious metaphysic is not a necessary precondition.[11] There has been a related argument as to whether the realist novel is not in some fundamental way opposed to tragedy.[12] Such arguments are complicated by the fact that the novel form has subsisted largely by assimilating, or giving an afterlife to, other genres such as epic, tragedy and comedy.[13] The question then arises whether the novel is preserving or dissolving these genres. At a generalised level arguments of this kind can be pretty arid but they can also highlight real tensions between the metaphysical premises of different genres. The significant tension in *Chronicle* can therefore be brought out by juxtaposing it with the two works with which it seems almost to invite comparison. These are Hardy's novel *Tess of the d'Urbevilles* (1891)and Lorca's poetic tragedy *Blood Wedding* (1933).

The detail of the warning note thrust under the Nasars' door but not found till too late points to the larger similarity of situation in Hardy's *Tess*. I have already remarked that the scientific, or at least scientistic, determinism of some nineteenth-century thought merged with an emotional fatalism and social pessimism to provide an ambiguous structure of feeling in much late nineteenth-century fiction. When Márquez' *Hundred Years* was compared with Conrad's *Nostromo* it was partly with a view to seeing how the brooding pessimism of Conrad's narrative has become more clearly a question *within* the narrative structure of *Hundred Years*. Yet even so Márquez was still far from offering any one-sided resolution of the question. The historical sweep and compression of his story leaves the question rather embedded consciously within it. In *Chronicle*, particularly when it is compared with *Tess*, we can see that the question is still ultimately enigmatic but it is brought into a sharper and more critical focus. For the real question is not the metaphysics of freedom *per se* so much as their possible use as an alibi for abnegation of responsibility. In this respect, at least, Márquez has in his generation a greater clarity of vision than Hardy had in his.

The magnificent social and psychological understanding of Hardy's novel is overlaid with an occasional rhetoric of tragic fatalism. Most readers have felt some falsity and straining in the 'poetic' and 'philosophical' strands which lead to the President of the Immortals. At the same time the power and truth of his central conception carries such moments and even imbues them with a nearly successful imaginative life. But whereas Hardy seeks to add a tragic and fatalistic aura around his novel, Márquez places precisely this tragic consciousness, and its attendant temptations for both characters and author, within the testing frame of his historical fiction. The point of the comparison is not to suggest that *Chronicle* is on balance a greater work than *Tess* but to bring out the particular quality and implication of Márquez' generic framings.

It is useful to pause in a similar spirit on the opposite comparison with Lorca's *Blood Wedding*. Like Márquez, Lorca started with a real-life occasion: a rather sordid killing arising from a wedding-night triangle. But unlike Márquez, Lorca refined away the journalistic elements of the occasion. His poetry at all times uses highly evocative, mutually isolated images which resist any too realistic accounting of their meaning. So here, Lorca enters dramatically into the particular historical culture and converts the episode into a universal passional statement. Although the audience is not assumed to be part of this culture, indeed precisely because the audience is assumed *not* to be part of it, we are able, as with ancient Greek drama, to participate imaginatively in a universal insight. Lorca's skill lies in the tact and consistency with which he is able to encompass the culturally specific context while keeping any too realistic consciousness outside his artistic frame.

We could say that Lorca's play achieves, and then maintains throughout, the gem-like purity of the Vicente poem which Márquez invokes only in his epigraph. Beside the pure intensity of Lorca, Márquez seems relatively loose and muddy. But this seems deliberate, as if Márquez, with his inveterately novelistic bias, wants to place the whole 'tragic' experience, together with its passional premises, within the questioning context of a realist fiction. And the difference is no doubt generational too, Márquez distrusts any grand or all-encompassing gesture.

The complementary danger here, artistically, is of a too merely debunking effect and a loss of the tragic consciousness which needs to heighten the whole. Or else the work may fall into that uncertainty of tone noted in *Tess*. For this reason it is crucial that the two narrative lenses of *Chronicle*, the tragic and the journalistic, should be mutually permeable. For while the narrator's investigative purpose is to question the 'tragic' interpretation of the events, it is also in turn irradiated by this. The narrator, after all, is a participant, and his enquiry illuminates, but does not ultimately explain, the enigma. In this respect, it is important to note that the logical hierarchy of narrative frames does not necessarily correspond to their relative dramatic power. Neither one quite controls the other. The ultimate effect of the historical outer frame is not to reduce the tragic consciousness to a diagnostic insight but to set it in an even more powerful and enigmatic relief.

Indeed, Márquez has allowed his narrator to divide the action into five sections suggestive of the five acts of a drama. Of course, the five sections do not directly mimic theatrical structure but then neither do they simply unfold the experience in a conventionally chronological way. Their spatialised retrospect combines the concentration of dramatic structure with the digressive spirit of narrative as the narrator continues to circle around the central enigma. As in *Hundred Years*, the first chapter, and the first sentence, give a synoptic statement of the whole. The subsequent chapters then circle in different ways around the same action, adding layers to our understanding. From the very opening sentence, the whole structure is a cunning combination of gradual narrative revelation: the story has, after all, great suspense, with a spatialised meditation on its meaning. In other words, the fundamental structure combines what for purposes of exposition I am calling the 'tragic' and the 'novelistic' consciousness. The novelistic is irradiated by the tragic while the tragic is constantly questioned and displaced by the novelistic.

To look at the work in the light of its underlying imaginative problems and strategies highlights the imaginative achievement. It also helps explain why another dimension of the story is to some extent its Achilles' heel. Márquez has remarked that he finally understood how to treat his central theme only when he realised that it was also a great love story. As in *Tess* too, it is the fact that the central couple do really love each other which lifts the story onto an appropriate plane of interest. The love that grows between Angela and Bayardo gives a sharper edge to the logic of the action and refines the central complex of feeling. Angela was pressured into the marriage against her will by her family, who were overcome not just by Bayardo's wealth and social power but also by the confident charm that goes with these. Only through the catastrophe of the wedding night does she realise his actual vulnerability, his genuine feeling for her, and the authenticity of his charm. She starts to fall in love with him at the point where he rejects her. Hence his rejection of her has more to it than the formality of wounded honour while she begins a process of self-knowledge, ultimately on behalf of both of them.

But what is immediately to be noted about the love theme of *Chronicle* in narrative terms is its carefully controlled indirection; its precise subordination to the theme of the killing. As I have observed several times, such indirection is the hallmark of Márquez' narrative skill yet on the present occasion it seems also to be a problem. For while the love of Angela and Bayardo is crucial in giving a different edge to the central situation it seems only partly assimilated artistically. Bayardo is necessarily a mystery to Angela and it makes sense that his rather commanding behaviour coupled with her resistance to him should work to create and preserve this mystery. But he remains, for this reason, too much of an external device for the reader too. As the fabulously wealthy, mysterious stranger he is inevitably a romántic extravagance for the reader and his return to Angela, after many years, with her dozens of letters preserved but still unopened, belongs to a different realm of fiction. We can feel Márquez pulling out the stops here as if to cover a weaker but necessary element in the narrative structure. And in terms of the preceding discussion, we can see why Márquez needs such tonal contrasts. It is as if the counter-term to the tragic cannot be simply the mundane and so Márquez is trying to invest his novelistic narrative with a compensatory, larger-than-life gesture. It is his equivalent of the President of the Immortals. By the same token, however, Márquez has a good understanding of why he needs this folkloric dimension and he is careful to keep it subordinate and contributory; a point which is incidentally highlighted by comparison with the filmed version of the book in which the courtship and reunion are given a disproportionate dramatic weight. In the novella these are firmly contained in the second and fourth, rather than in the first and the final, sections.

There are further reasons for the larger-than-life, incipiently folkloric, presentation of Bayardo. It is a way of making him part of the imaginative medium of the novella at the level of personal psychology. I have already observed several times how Márquez rarely gives fully omniscient access to the inner lives of his characters and in *Chronicle* this technique is dramatically justified by the convention of the enquiring narrator who can only proceed by inference. The two other major figures, Angela and Santiago, remain enigmatic because of the uncertainty as to whether Angela's accusation is truthful.

By contrast, we feel that Márquez has to work up an aura of mystery around Bayardo. Yet he also justifies this to a large degree by presenting Bayardo as a figure who has had this striking effect on the small town population; his aura of mystery is strictly his impact on the local imagination. The larger logic of this in turn is that Márquez' interest ultimately lies not in the individual psychology of the characters so much as in the underlying cultural structures that largely determine their lives. The slightly two-dimensional quality of Bayardo is a way of signalling and controlling this focus of interest.

Like much Latin American fiction, the story shows a popular consciousness which is doubly bereft in that it falls disastrously between cultures. The notions of sexual honour held by Bayardo and the Vicarios, and largely accepted by the townsfolk, seem damagingly anachronistic, yet the modern systems of law and religion fail in just as signal a way to address the people's needs. The whole story takes place under the sign of the cross but only in the form of the bishop's empty blessing from the boat. The bishop fails even to stop at the town yet he has already provided much of the distraction that has allowed the catastrophe to build up unimpeded. This cultural uncertainty of inhabiting different worlds simultaneously yet neither of them completely and coherently is appropriately figured by the framing of an ancient, tragic fatalism within the modern-day questioning of an investigating journalist. The travelled narrator understands, but cannot simultaneously inhabit, both worlds. Whereas the narrative of *Hundred Years* nostalgically adopted the folkloric voice, in *Chronicle* they stand in a more quizzical tension.

The same uncertain duality is reflected in the opacity of virtually all the other characters to the narrator and to us. We don't know exactly what they are thinking, or even how they think. The Vicario brothers are most strikingly representative of this divided culture in their half-conscious appeal to be rescued from their world. And by making them twins, with an almost collective psyche, Márquez has neatly protected their inner life, or their apparent absence of introspection, from the possible impact of authorial omniscience while at the same time strongly communicating their inner ambivalence. Instead of an integral consciousness which might experience itself introspectively as divided we have initially one brother who wants to perform the revenge and one who is reluctant. And then, when it appears that honour no longer requires them to go through with the killing, they reverse roles as the other becomes insistent. One is clearly motivated more externally by the code of honour while the other, though slow to arouse on that score, is then impossible to stop. The obligation of revenge has now been internalised as a personal motive which is perhaps all it can be for him. The retrospective narration naturalises this external presentation of the brothers while highlighting their ambivalence.

If Márquez' concern lies in the underlying cultural functions and forces rather than in individual motivations, he also leads us to peer into deeper mysteries even than the sociological. The whole action takes place in the spring and Santiago's surname 'Nasar' isolates him as an Arab. The highly ambivalent warning 'Por ahí no, turco' (p. 149) / 'Not this way, Turk!' (p. 117) is the last human utterance he hears before his death. His name is also a reminder of the most famous Nazarene, Christ, whose cruel and scandalous death was also eminently foretold and chronicled. And Christ's death was similarly the outcome, in some ambiguously conniving way, of the whole community and culture in which it occurred. The Christ analogy, however, should not be pushed too far, if only because Márquez himself has the tact not to do so and Christ 'symbolism' can too easily be a cheap bid for significance in fiction. But more importantly, Márquez' final 'scene' of the killing is much more elusively suggestive. The Christian echo acts rather as an anthropological pointer to there being, or there perhaps being, something deep and communal at stake in the killing while leaving quite open the question of its possible meanings.

The killing is a public spectacle in the main square of the town. It implicitly involves the community as a whole, who are assembled like choric witnesses for this last act. Without ceasing to understand all this in modern ethical, social and psychological terms we also sense that some deeper nerve has been touched, some ancient stratum of feeling that might lie behind blood sacrifice, the earliest origins of tragedy, or indeed of the Mass or an 'auto-da-fe'. There is no question of glorifying violence here, or of sentimental primitivism. It is rather an example of the greater willingness of Latin American writers to acknowledge, and thus be in a position more truly to question, the 'instinct' to violence within the self and the culture.[14] Once again, the blend of ancient tragic spectacle and a modern journalistic viewpoint opens further levels of questioning. Is the event revelatory of some fundamental passional reality; is it an atavistic survival; or is it merely an arbitrary concatenation of chance and folly?

The Christ motive is thus more scattered than patterned in the book. As an only half suggested significance, it is as much centrifugal as centripetal. The twins, Pablo and Pedro, are named after the two greatest disciples who had nonetheless respectively persecuted and denied Christ. But the Vicario brothers undergo no such conversion. These self-appointed ministers of vengeance serve no Christian purpose. At the same time, the general deflection of the Christian parallel has its more positive side in so far as, through Santiago's death which has put such a stamp of apparent finality on the disaster of her marriage, it is his possible betrayer, Angela, who undergoes an effective rebirth.

Angela, indeed, seems to be the only character, apart from the shadowy Bayardo, who really grows in the light of her experience and this leads to a final Marquesian emphasis. For what saves Angela is not Christian faith, by which she has not been well served, but her twin discovery of love and writing. Indeed, a Christian echo is used to reinforce the point when she consciously rejects her former ethic as she sees it embodied in her pious mother whose name, of course, is as emblematic as those of Galdos' Doña Perfecta and Lorca's Bernarda Alba.[15]

> Pura Vicario había acabado de beber, se secó los labios con la manga y le sonrió desde el mostrador con los lentes nuevos. En esa sonrisa, por primera vez desde su nacimiento, Angela Vicario la vio tal como era: una pobre mujer consagrada al *culto* de sus defectos. 'Mierda', se dijo. Estaba tan trastornada, que hizo todo el viaje de regreso cantando en voz alta, y se tiró en la cama a llorar *durante tres días*.
> *Nació de nuevo.* (p. 121)

> Pura Vicario had finished drinking, dried her lips on her sleeve, and smiled at her from the counter with her new glasses. In that smile, for the first time since she was born, Angela Vicario saw her as she was: a poor woman devoted to the *cult* of her defects. 'Shit,' she said to herself. She was so shattered she spent the whole return trip singing out loud, and threw herself on her bed to weep *for three days*.
> *She was reborn.* (p. 93 my emphases)

It is from this moment that her love for Bayardo becomes obsessive and she starts to write her series of letters to him. Once again, as in Márquez' earlier fiction, the need to speak out is an ungovernable, almost physical urge which also acquires, in its written form, some special inflections.

At this point of conversion, Angela transcends the fatalistic consciousness that has so damagingly pervaded the action so far. The true enemy of freedom, after all, is not fate but fatalism. Yet as she becomes 'dueña por primera vez de su destino' (p. 122) / 'mistress of her fate for the first time' (p. 94) she also realises the passional force to which she has now abandoned herself. Her new freedom is locked in conflict with obsession.

Se volvió lúcida, imperiosa, maestra de su albedrío, y volvió a ser virgen sólo para eĺ, y no reconoció otra autoridad que la suya ni más servidumbre que la de su obsesión. (p. 122)

She became clear-headed, imperious, mistress of her own will, and she became a virgin again just for him, and recognized no authority other than her own nor any other service than that of her obsession. (p. 94)

Her condition, pointed up by the reference to virginity, is almost a mirror image of her earlier state, or of her mother's. But it is now a struggle for recognition and fulfilment of feeling rather than repression of it, and within this struggle her writing performs a crucial function. By pouring her madness into writing she saves herself from succumbing to it in life. And although her conscious purpose is always to move Bayardo, we recognise, as with Samuel Richardson's letter-writing heroines, that the writing is performing a necessary function for her almost irrespective of whether it will actually be read. The act of writing is internally liberating and empowering even in a situation of external oppression. Many novelists have used the female viewpoint because the woman's relative lack of social power meant that even if she had the intrinsic moral authority of Richardson's Clarissa Harlowe or Jane Austen's Emma Woodhouse she was obliged to exercise it through indirect means based on a more complete and inward understanding of what was going on around her. Like novelists, such figures have a power of understanding in an inverse ratio to their power of action. And so Angela remains pretty marginalised as a character but she is closest to an authorial understanding and preserves a sphinx-like reserve towards the overtly authorial figure of the narrator.

As she tells the narrator, given that Bayardo seemed so 'insensible a su delirio. Era como escribirle a nadie (p. 123) / 'insensible to her delirium, it was like writing to nobody'. (p. 95) And if the idea of writing to an imagined reader begins to suggest the situation of a novelist, the parallel is borne out by the substance and tone of the letters. They become increasingly imaginative:

Al principio fueron esquelas de compromiso, después fueron papelitos de amante furtiva, billetes perfumados de novia fugaz, memoriales de negocios, documentos de amor, y por último fueron las cartas indignas de una sposa abandonada que se inventaba enfermedades crueles para obligarlo a volver. (p. 123)

At first they were a fiancée's messages, then they were little missives as from a secret lover, perfumed cards from a hidden sweetheart, business letters, love documents, and finally the indignant letters of an abandoned wife inventing cruel illnesses to make him return. (p. 95)

And she varies the tone on intrinsic and expressive rather than referential grounds:

En ocasiones, cansada de llorar, se burlaba de su propria locura. (p. 123)

On occasion, tired of weeping, she would make fun of her own madness. (p. 95)

In Cervantes, it is frequently the women who can make fun of madness and are able to control it, and their deluded menfolk too, through the beneficient means of fiction.[16] So here, whereas her brothers got caught in the fiction of their revenge, Angela uses fiction as a means of escape from the emotional entrapment of an atavistic code. Angela's writing is fictional but is not merely sublimative. It is a means of self-recognition as well as emotional catharsis.

The most passionate and desperate of her letters speaks directly of her sexual desire:

Le habló de las lacras eternas que el' había dejado en su cuerpo, de la sal de su lengua, de la trilla de fuego de su verga africana. (pp. 123–4)

She told him of the eternal scars he had left on her body, of the salt of his tongue, and of the burning mark of his African rod. (p. 95)

The last phrase is particularly suggestive in that it links Bayardo to Santiago who is also of African descent. It may be that in choosing to name Santiago as her seducer Angela was finding, half unconsciously, another predatory and dominating male on whom to direct her resentment of Bayardo. After all, although the confusion of her behaviour was always comprehensible and hardly blamable, her handling of the wedding-night was effectively 'designed' to do the maximum damage to Bayardo. Despite advice, she neither told him the truth nor took the customary steps to protect him from the knowledge.

But having punctured Bayardo's pride she now recognises her own prejudice and not only expresses desire for his maleness but does so in a deliberately male imagery. Her culminating fiction is to offer herself to him as the woman of a classically male projection. In fact, in its context of the quasi-fictional emotional release of letter writing, her phrasing seems to challenge the rather self-serving cliché of some feminist criticism that the pen is a form of penis. As her acculturated barriers drop away in writing, she becomes, in a quite simple and proper sense, a woman who wants a penis: her husband's.

But the pen, in whomever's hands, can be penetrative. What matters is the spirit in which it is handled and this is the question on which Márquez has his eye. Angela's piled-up letters to Bayardo are eventually returned by him unopened but the gesture is now one of love and acceptance. The episode has a negative echo in Santiago's chestful of 'cartas sin amor' (p. 147) / 'loveless letters' (p. 115) to Flora Miguel. This latter phrase inverts the expression 'love letters' and, in the broader context created by Angela's epistolary fictions, it reinforces John Bayley's more general argument in *The Characters of Love* that the writing of worthwhile fiction has always in some sense to be an act of love.[17] Angela's writing extends the thread of concern for questions of fiction and truth which was evident in the lampoons, graffiti and gossip of earlier tales. This concern has now been inflected towards love rather than politics but it continues to provide a naturalised focus within the book for recognitions about the nature of fiction. Fictional understanding is an act of love as well as truth-telling.

So too, we might say that, within the terms of the narrative, the fictive historian is also the voice of the fiction. And his desire to understand the 'meaning' of the events has for us a metaphysical inflection beyond his own purpose of establishing an historical causality. While some characters in the book seem to be caught within their own fictions, the narrator, like Angela, is using fiction as a means of understanding. His mother is an embodiment of this function.

She has, like Márquez in Caracas, an uncanny ability to anticipate what is going to happen, not through some magical ability but through her sympathetic attentiveness to what is going on around her. Unfortunately, she was not able to anticipate the disaster of the present tale, perhaps because she was not close enough to the principals. As it happens, she too writes letters although she hesitates to commit to writing her final unease about Bayardo. But an earlier remark affirming his fundamentally good character invites the following comment from the narrator.

> . . . mi madre suele hacer esa clase de precisiones superfluas cuando quiere llegar al fondo de las cosas. (p. 39)

> . . . my mother usually goes into that kind of superfluous detail when she wants to get to the bottom of things. (p. 26)

It is a nice touch. Her son has learnt, at least when listening to her, that he must attend to the 'superfluous' in order to arrive at the essential. Márquez' own fiction constantly uses this trick of apparent, and apparently artless, indirection. More broadly, the whole method of fiction, and of realist fiction particularly, lies in this equivocation about the superfluous.

In the present tale, which is second cousin to the detective story, there is an especially close and ironic focus on the question of the essential and the superfluous. The story itself is constructed with a close logic in which we soon recognise that nothing is superfluous. Yet at the level of events it is part of the point that most of the specific details of the action should stand under the sign of the superfluous or the arbitrary. So many of them need not have happened. In this way, everything in the story seems at once arbitrary and essential. And this, of course, points to the central enigma of whether fate or chance, tragedy or mess, lies at the 'bottom of things' for us.

Once again, Márquez' tale is pervaded with a subtly sub-textual self-consciousness. Angela's letters, the narrator's mother and the narrator's own meditations all contribute to this, as does the incidental choice of terms such as when Angela replies to the investigator's direct question about Santiago's guilt saying 'Fue mi autor' (p. 131) / 'he was my author' (p. 101) in which the awkwardness of the English (meaning 'he was the author of my misfortunes') brings out the careful inflection of the Spanish. Like Richardson's heroines, Angela struggles to be her own author.

In view of this, it is not surprising that the relation of love, writing and an 'authorial' command of one's own experience should be the overt themes of Márquez' next novel. And as he goes on to make love his central theme, he seems to require, quite consciously, a different kind of fiction.

7

Not Flaubert's Parrot: *Love in the Time of Cholera*

Although Márquez' next novel keeps the familiar theme of time in its title, it now gives first place to the word 'love'. It tells, in a leisurely and protracted series of flashbacks, the story of the life-long love of the illegitimate, and once poor, Florentino Ariza for Fermina Daza. Their teenage love had been sustained largely by his letters as she was sent away by her ambitious father. But when they suddenly met after this long separation, her 'illusion' of love, as she then saw it, was immediately dispelled. She rejected him to marry, although also after a period of rejection, the socially well-placed doctor Juvenal Urbino, who was already some thirty years old. Much of the book is taken up with a study of this marriage and of the myriad affairs by which Florentino tries to fill the space left by Fermina while waiting one day to possess her. The present action of the novel opens on the day of Dr Urbino's sudden death, in his eighties, while trying to retrieve his escaped parrot. His death allows Florentino to resume his courtship of Fermina. This time he is eventually successful and the story ends with them sailing up and down the Magdalena river, isolated by a cholera flag, on a boat owned by the steamship company of which Florentino is now the president. It ends, that is to say, with a romantic gesture for which it is hard to imagine the realistic outcome.

Cholera is, in short, a love story and it is handled as if the love motif of *Chronicle* had now expanded to require a book of its own. This is not just a matter of space, or even of narrative proportion. The love story in *Chronicle* seemed to need a different mode of fiction and part of the interest of *Cholera* is not only to develop this possibility but implicitly to reflect upon and justify it. The relationship between the two books, in other words, is a striking instance of an increasingly evident feature of Márquez' *œuvre*. One book seems partly to give birth to another which then goes on in turn to develop such a distinctive life of its own that it represents, if not a critique of the preceding work, then a significantly new vantage point from which to see it.

Cholera is most briefly, and perhaps most adequately, described as a love story. For the homely populism of the phrase is part of the book's own characteristic note. Yet the very familiarity and apparent simplicity of this phrase, indeed its nearness to cliché, present special problems of value and attention. That is why Márquez does not just seek to tell a popular love story; he sets out at the same time a sophisticated vindication of his subject and its form. This consists largely of a sustained meditation on both terms, 'love' *and* 'story', and on the relationship between them. But Márquez' also places this meditation within a wide-ranging, if implicit, context of literary history. The book is full of narrative elements which are in the first instance simply part of the action but which at the same time provide a continuous, discreet means of self-reference on the part of the fiction by which it defines and locates itself against some of the prestigious achievements, and widely accepted criteria, of earlier modern literature.

The figure who provides the significant reference point here is Flaubert, although what is strictly at stake is not so much Flaubert himself as his myth. It is Flaubert's prestigious impact on modern literary thinking and most especially his ideal of an impersonally technical control by which the ineradicable human impulse to romance is contained within an ironically detached, aestheticised nihilism. The form is inseparable from the vision. It is appropriate as well as ironic that Julian Barnes' *Flaubert's Parrot* (1984), with its witty and telling reaffirmation of the Flaubertian spirit, and its parenthetic swipe at 'magical realism', should have been published only a year before *Cholera* (1985). For *Cholera* offers a sustained, if side-long, challenge to the Flaubertian spirit.

I say 'side-long' because the direct allusions to Flaubert are the merest hints; anything more overt might have turned the novel into an elite intra-literary game rather than the popular and independently accessible work it actually is. Hence there is a passing reference to Florentino' Ariza's 'educación sentimental' / 'sentimental education'.[1] And the local hospital is named after St. Julian the Hospitaler (pp. 182, 337 / pp. 125, 234). But once our attention is focused, we notice that a character who has an intense relationship with a parrot dies looking at it. And then we see the further significance of having at the centre of the story a study of the prosaic marriage of a provincial doctor and of his wife's suppressed romanticism. Of course, Dr Urbino and Fermina are a far cry from Charles and Emma Bovary but what the marriages have in common is their mundane representativeness as pointed up by the narrative in each case. The differences in personal quality are part of the force of the comparison. These differences challenge the basis of Flaubertian representativeness just as Márquez brings a fresh light to the Flaubertian use of the cliché.

In fact, indirection characterises the book more generally than just in the sidelong relation to Flaubert. Indirection has now become its dominant technical strategy and, we might almost say, its subject matter. For the narrative constantly sneaks up on the reader just as the character's emotions are constantly taking them by surprise. It is worth pausing on this aspect of the narrative before pursuing the implication of the Flaubertian allusions.

As has been noted several times, Márquez has always used techniques of indirection. The technical devices listed by Vargas Llosa are for the most part different forms of narrative obliqueness. In *Cholera*, however, these seem even more accentuated and humorously shared with the reader. For example, a favourite Marquesian effect has always been to introduce new material as if it were already known to the reader. Even an episode as important as the massacre of the strikers in *Hundred Years* is edged into the narrative in this way. Very often the effect, as in *Hundred Years*, can be to reinforce the spatialised chronology of the narrative. The story is told as if it were already within our possession. The technique can also disguise the importance of what is being introduced. To speak of something as if we already knew all about it is to imply that the topic does not need further explanation.

In *Cholera*, Márquez is less concerned to create the compressed and mythic spatialising of time which he sought in *Hundred Years* but he is still concerned to dramatise the interrelations of emotion and time. Time both changes, and is unable to change, Florentino's love. Like the colonel of *No One Writes*, Florentino affirms a Quixotic value by his heroic endurance. At the beginning of his love for Fermina, Florentino is unaware that it will not be consummated till nearly the end of their lives; that his life is going literally to enact what would normally be a poetic hyperbole. And in a complementary way, Dr Urbino does not know at the beginning of the novel that this is to be his last day. Here Márquez reverses the device of apparently foretelling Col. Aureliano Buendía's death by firing squad. The opening chapter has several references to the doctor's death which make us suppose it to be still a long way off, as in:

... dictó en la Escuela de Medicina todos las días de lunes a sábado, a las ocho en punto, hasta la víspera de su muerte. (p. 21)

... he taught at the School of Medicine every morning, from Monday through Saturday, at eight o'clock punctually, until the day before his death. (p. 12)

We are unlikely at first to realise that this *is* the day of his death and particularly since this account of *his* own day is being placed in evident contrast, and in apparent narrative subordination, to that of his friend, the aptly named Jeremiah de Saint-Amour, who has foretold and arranged his own death for that very day. In the same opening chapter, Dr Urbino's 'wife' and the parrot are also introduced with a comparably deceptive casualness. We do not know what principally to focus on in this opening chapter, just as the characters do not know what is going to prove most important in their lives. The whole narrative unfolds in a comparably ambiguous way creating a curious effect of leisurely suspense or suspenseful leisure. The central love affair is finally developed only at the very end of the novel and depends entirely on this anterior effect of constant distraction. The main body of the book is a narrative *tour de force* in simply filling the space between youth and age. In the abstract, this formula is a Beckettian one, but the Marquesian emphasis is on the preciousness rather than the emptiness of time. The book's delight in its own narrative bravura enacts its theme of enjoyment.

The mixture of suspense and leisure in the narrative is in the first instance, therefore, a way of enforcing a *carpe diem* recognition. But it does so by constantly revealing the processes by which everyday life blunts and distracts from this romantic wisdom. Proust saw habit as the great deadener. Márquez' narration constantly enacts an enjoyment of the momentary texture of experience while tripping us up if we are not on the alert for sudden changes. In this respect it reflects the emotional lives of the characters. The emotional life is volatile and it is overlaid with habit and rationalisation so that its subterranean current is often undetected. Or else when this does come to the surface, it is not understood. Fermina's response to her disgraced father's death is a case in point:

> Fermina Daza no pudo reprimir un suspiro de alivio cuando le llegó la noticia de la muerte, y no le guardó luto para evitar preguntas, pero durante varios meses lloraba con una rabia sorda sin saber por qué cuando se encerraba a fumar en el baño, y era que lloraba por el. (pp. 308–9)

> Fermina Daza could not repress a sigh of relief when the news of his death came and in order to avoid questions she did not wear mourning, but for several months she wept with dumb fury without knowing why when she locked herself in the bathroom to smoke, and it was because she was crying for him. (p. 215)

As has been seen in several previous works, Márquez frequently withholds omniscient insight into his characters. In this book he suggests more directly the unknowability of true feeling to simple introspection and the corresponding impossibility of summing up a relationship. This recognition is crucial to the portrayal of the Urbinos' marriage. Apart from anything else, the novel is a remarkable, if humorous, treatment of marriage but it is so because this marriage, and marriage in general, are both understood in the light of this fundamental recognition. In *Chronicle*, the narrator engaged the difficulty of understanding the mentality of a different culture. To an important extent, every long-term marriage develops its own culture which no outsider can ever be sure to have penetrated.

From one point of view the marriage of Dr Urbino and Fermina is merely a fifty-year interruption of Florentino's courtship. And the flashback technique of the narrative frankly treats it as such. Yet it also proves to be the route, and perhaps the necessary route, to the final romance, since both characters develop importantly through their experiences during this period. It is the marriage that gives Fermina her realistic appreciation of romance. And from this point of view it is important that the story should give the marriage its proper weight. It is not merely an obstacle. What we most come away with is a sense of its absolute resistance to any summary statement of its emotional quality or success. It is a very average sort of a marriage seen with clear, but not cynical, eyes. The relationship has been passionate, affectionate, boring, angry and desperate. But none of these sums it up. It presents no easy counter-term to the subsequent romance and it thereby gives a greater force, and testing, to the romance when it comes. In this novel, of course, the counter-term to 'romance' is not 'marriage' but 'age'. As the title suggests, the lovers triumph over time.[2]

In acknowledging this weight and complexity in the Urbinos' marriage, Marquez is affirming such a significance in marriage *per se*. For the specific internal chemistry of the Urbinos' marriage suggests something about the nature of marriage at large. In the classic tradition of romantic love, passion was necessarily adulterous.[3] Marriage has always for that reason been a central theme of the novel because it represents the point of tension, for good or ill, between personal fulfilment and the requirements of the social order. That was the structural function of marriage in the nineteenth-century novel of which *Madame Bovary* is a classic instance.[4] But in this connection it is suggestive that, whereas Flaubert's title *Madame Bovary* refers to the former Emma Roualt purely by her married name, Fermina Daza, partly because of the different Hispanic conventions, continues to be referred to in the narrative by her personal and maiden names. In the twentieth century marriage has become more a matter of personal fulfilment, or otherwise, with less weight given to its meaning as a social institution. But wherever such a modern marriage continues to represent a lifetime commitment, it can actually embody the workings of the reality principle even more strongly and subtly than did the old sense of a social institution.

For the social institution represented an impersonal order to which an individual would give a personal inflection but which individuals did not create and could not significantly modify. The institution itself could therefore be held responsible for the happiness or otherwise of those inside it. But with the progressive weakening of the social institution, marriage has acquired an almost unique value in being a closed system in which two individuals live with the continuing, direct consequences of their own personalities. A lifetime's career in teaching, for example, may wreak untold damage, if only that of wasted time, on generations of students, but the perpetrator may remain happily unconscious because the students continually go away. Any comeback is only temporary. In a marriage, by contrast, the comeback is both short-term and long-term; it expresses itself at varying levels of consciousness; and above all it is inescapable as long as the marriage lasts.

The Urbino's marriage lasts into the new century and Márquez' presentation of it catches this intimate working of the reality principle as the interaction of two individuals defining and creating each other within a closed system. His humour brings out the structural dimension of this as well as the immediately personal, and often painful, feeling. At the same time, of course, the humour is a distancing device. The marriage is not the ultimate subject of the book. But he nonetheless communicates the rounded and complex workings of a marriage with an insider's knowledge in a way that I doubt Flaubert could. Flaubert could understand it very well in his own way, which was as an outsider. The bachelorhood of Flaubert is as relevant to his literary vision as is that of James or Turgenev. And by the same token, Márquez' own long marriage seems to have been an importantly formative precondition of his imaginative world just as, more obviously, D. H. Lawrence's was. Of course, this is not simply to attribute all such effects to marriage *per se*. It depends on the individuals' being open to its possibilities. If Flaubert had married he would undoubtedly, like many another, have remained essentially a bachelor and he was wise not to inflict this fate on a woman. That was part of the sense in which he *did* understand the question very well from his own point of view.

There is something larger at stake, therefore, in the volatility of the Urbino marriage in contrast to the enclosure of the Bovary's. Of course, in an immediate sense the two marriages are incomparable because the authors are writing about different characters and for different purposes. But in a more significant underlying sense the characters are precisely the products of these different artistic and personal visions. With his French suspicion of feeling and romance, Flaubert sardonically traces the inextricability of the romantic impulse in the lives of his major characters and implicitly identifies its only proper expression as being in the art of the book itself. Márquez has a more English sense of the necessary, and proper, interaction of feeling and world so that the important question is rather to discriminate the quality of the feelings. It is as if Márquez were seeking to write something more like an English novel of moral and emotional growth while staying within Flaubert's terms. Only in this way could he make fully conscious and pertinent the challenge to the Flaubertian spirit. Henry James once remarked, after one of his visits to Flaubert's literary circle, how no one present was aware that George Eliot's *Daniel Deronda* had just been published and how none of them would have understood the significance of the event if they had been told of it.[5] Hence Márquez deliberately invokes Flaubert's terms and not least by keeping the general categories of 'reality' and 'romance' distinct in the reader's mind.

The text is at all times humorously aware both of the fundamental struggle between romance and reality and of their inextricability. This is apparent in the young Florentino's business letters:

> . . . Florentino Ariza escribía cualquier cosa con tanta pasión, que hasta los documentos oficiales parecían de amor. Los manifiestos de embarque le salían rimados por mucho que se esforzara en evitarlo, y las cartas comerciales de rutina tenían un aliento lírico que les restaba autoridad. (p. 246)

> . . . Florentino Ariza would write anything with so much passion that even official documents seemed to be about love. His bills of lading came out in rhyme however he tried to avoid it, and routine business letters had a lyrical air that undermined their authority. (p. 171)

And this initial statement of the theme is answered much later when the mature Florentino begins to have some success in wooing the widowed Fermina with a different kind of letter:

> Era una carta de seis pliegos que no tenía nada que ver con ninguna otra que hubiera escrito alguna vez. No tenía ni el tono, ni el estilo, ni el soplo retórico de los primero años del amor, y su argumento era tan racional y bien medido, que el perfume de una gardenia hubiera sido un exabrupto. En cierto modo, fue la aproximación más acertada de las cartas mercantiles que nunca pudo hacer. (p. 424)

> It was a six-page letter, quite unlike any he had ever written before. It did not have the tone, the style, or the rhetorical air of his early years of love, and his argument was so rational and measured that the scent of a gardenia would have been out of place. In a way, it was his closest approximation to the business letters he had never been able to write. (p. 296)

While we see that Florentino has changed, the continuity of the business letter theme allows us also to see that this later style is only a transposition of the same melody. The youthful romance is not transcended so much as transformed.

Márquez enjoys tracing the all-pervading nature of romance whereby it constantly subverts and assimilates its apparent opposites. At one point, as his lover Angeles Alfaro, the young girl who plays the cello naked, leaves on the boat for good, Florentino comes to recognise that 'se puede estar enamorado dc varias personas a la vez, y de todas con el mismo dolor, sin traicionar a ninguna' (pp. 393–4) / ' . . . one can be in love with several people at the same time, and feel the same anguish for each, without betraying any of them' (p. 274) Whereupon he remarks as a general dictum: '"El corazón tiene más cuartos que un hotel de putas"' / 'The heart has more rooms than a whorehouse'.[6] He is momentarily shocked by this recognition but the narrative is not and, sure enough, ' . . . no bien había desaparecido el barco en la línea de la horizonte, cuando ya el recuerdo de Fermina Daza había vuelto a ocupar su espacio total' / ' . . . no sooner had the ship disappeared over the horizon, than the memory of Fermina Daza once again filled all his space'. Romantic love, it has already been remarked, is not essentially an ethical impulse. As Stendhal bluntly put it: 'True passion is a selfish thing'.[7] The remark about the heart and the whorehouse is an earthy way of putting what the narrative at large seems to bear out: that love is resilient, elastic, volatile and multiple. The image is even perhaps a distant cousin of 'My Father's house has many mansions' and it is worth remarking in passing that the acceptance of multiplicity is an artistic, as well as a psychological, principle. The solitude of Melquiades, and of the 'lonely God' of *In Evil Hour*, arose not from the absence, so much as the even-handed multiplicity, of their relations with humankind at large.

That at least is the more negative side of the equation. But this book constantly suggests the more positive interrelations of 'love' and 'fiction' which may lurk in the common expression 'love story'. Love may be an archetypal subject of fiction partly because it has a strong element of the fictional in its own constitution. Hence, where the anti-romantic tradition from Cervantes through Flaubert to Nabokov has used the elements of fiction to expose romance, Márquez rather delights in the inextricable working of the fictional within love. Florentino, for example, becomes a scribe of love, drawing on his own feelings to compose love letters for others.

He then finds himself conducting both sides of a correspondence which leads to a marriage and a child. This is the opposite joke to Flaubert's construction of a love conversation between Emma Bovary and Leon out of the clichés he sardonically amassed for his *Dictionary of Received Ideas*. In the case of Márquez' young couple, at least for all we know to the contrary, the genuineness of the feeling overrides and survives the artificiality of the occasion. The difference is partly an acceptance of language, even popular and clichéd language, as being independent of the feeling invested in it rather than as necessarily debasing the feeling in the expression. In so far as it remained within the Flaubertian orbit, much modern literature showed an unassuagable nostalgia for the genuinely popular touch. Joyce placed the common man at the centre of his work but could not be said simply to write for him. Márquez, for all his patrician spirit, has increasingly sought the popular note. This book is his most striking attempt to square the circle; to write a genuinely popular and accessible romance while maintaining, if only to challenge, the sophistication of a high modernist consciousness.

So, for example, as the final romance develops, Fermina becomes a fan of soap operas; a genre well known for its naïve equivocation with real life and its tendency to identify the performers with their parts. With a typical Marquesian effect, she listens to these interspersed with the real news which is how she hears the report of the elderly couple whose murder reveals them to have been clandestine lovers for forty years despite their each having a stable and fruitful marriage. The news item reduces Fermina to tears as the soap operas, which are designed to play on the feelings, do not, for it is in the fate of this couple that Fermina and Florentina recognise their potential selves. By intermingling the 'real' world of his fiction with that of soap opera, Márquez is not merely endorsing his heroine's love of soap operas, he is presenting his own story as a superior version of the genre. Superior, that is to say, but not condescending. Soap opera may be an undemanding form but Márquez feels no need to distance himself from it for the points of commonality are ultimately much greater than those of difference. In the 1980s Márquez was increasingly fascinated by the potential power of this phenomenally popular form. As he says, more people watch a soap opera in one night than have ever read his books.[8]

In short, Márquez is writing a popular romance which seeks to vindicate itself with a sophisticated literary historical self-consciousness. He fully acknowledges the projective and illusory nature of romantic love, what Stendhal called 'crystallisation'.[9] The teenage love of Fermina and Florentino is ended abruptly when she suddenly sees his prosaic reality close up and feels 'el abismo del desencanto' (p. 155) / 'the abyss of disenchantment' (p. 106). This echoes the puzzled recognition of Proust's Swann that Odette, the object of his formerly consuming passion, was not even his 'type'. But just as Proust's novel goes on to absorb this Flaubertian recognition into a more complex aesthetic vision of 'paradise' as an imaginative construct won from time, so Florentino's obstinate persistence is to effect a comparable change in the nature of feeling through time and with the help of his fictional imagination.

Perhaps that is why Proust is mentioned, but only obliquely, in the text (p. 172 / p. 118). For although its tone and ambition are so different, this is Márquez' most Proustian novel. The Proustian experience is transposed into the key of Márquez. There were Proustian echoes, for example, in *Hundred Years* but they were seen mainly in a critical light as part of the Buendía's insidious nostalgia. In *Cholera*, on the other hand, romantic nostalgia is more sympathetically treated and indeed the increasing nostalgia of Fermina for her youth even before being newly won over by Florentino is an important, unconscious step towards their late-flowering love. Without the elaborate metaphysics of love and imagination through which Proust constructs his final paradisal vision, their late affair has a comparable basis in recovered emotion and a consciously challenging transcendence of immediate reality. And likewise, as with Proust, there has been a conscious quest for the romantic experience on the part of the central male character while the true route to that experience proves to have been a process taking place largely outside of consciousness or will.

Márquez' carefully considered privileging of the romantic experience is further offset by his chosen counter-term of 'cholera'. Throughout his *œuvre* Márquez has used the technique of parenthetical reference which Vargas Llosa calls the 'caja china' or Chinese box. In other words, he imparts crucial information *a propos* of something else. In the early novellas especially, the horrors of the political situation were commonly revealed in this casual way, as in the remark that the funeral at the beginning of *No One Writes* was the first death by natural causes in ten years. The effect of this technique as used earlier was, of course, to increase our sense of such horrors. The present novel is likewise full of references to the civil wars and, one might think, the more tellingly so in so far as these references extend throughout the long lifetimes of the principal characters. But the actual effect is the reverse of this. We are rather struck by how little the essential lives of these characters are affected by political conditions and the long-standing nature of these conditions makes them appear to be rather one of the immovable conditions of life. This seems to be the principal function of the cholera motif. It metaphorically absorbs references to civil violence into a natural scourge; a scourge that might ideally be cured but is primarily to be understood as an aspect of the human condition at large. If this particular condition were removed, that is to say, the general nature of human existence would not be significantly altered. The supreme value of love would still be subject to time and mortality. This is the viewpoint from which Florentino's 'indiferencia política rayaba los límites de lo absoluto' (p. 388) / 'indifference to politics approached the limits of the absolute' (p. 270). Love, in short, will always be in the time of cholera; an implication which is clearer in the Spanish title where the 'times' of cholera are in an indefinite and recurrent plural.

But there is a further, more intrinsic, reason for this inescapability of conditions which is that love itself stands in no simple opposition to cholera. Indeed, it promotes cholera. For if the image of cholera assimilates war to human mortality at large, it also encompasses the dangerous fever of love. Hence, when Florentino is first in love,

> ... su madre se aterrorizó porque su estado no se parecía a los desórdenes del amor sino a los estragos del cólera. (p. 97)

> ... his mother was terrified because his condition did not seem like the pangs of love so much as the ravages of cholera. (p. 65)

And late in life, as her memory became confused, she

> ... solía decir: 'De lo único que mi hijo ha estado enfermo es del cólera.' Confundía el cólera con el amor, por supuesto, desde mucho antes de que se embrollara la memoria. (p. 320)

> ... used to say: 'The only disease my son ever had was cholera.' She was confusing cholera with love, of course, long before her memory became muddled. (p. 222)

Not only is love in itself a form of cholera, but Florentino images his courtship as a military campaign. In other words, the apparently polar oppositions are increasingly complexified as a double action takes place. On the one hand, cholera is a collective and distancing image for all that stands in opposition to romance. In that respect it is potentially undiscriminating and sentimental. On the other hand, romantic love is also part of the disease. We have already noted that the romantic impulse is distinct from the ethical and it should be remembered that Florentino's affairs have cost the lives of two of the women concerned. Hence, when the lovers finally hit on the idea of protecting their romantic isolation by sailing under the flag of cholera there is a multi-layered appropriateness in the gesture. They *are* in the grip of a dangerous contagion.

The novel's affirmation of romance, then, is in the face not just of a hostile or prosaic world, but of the darker side of romance itself. In this respect, the peculiar triumph of the book is its control of tone. It affirms a permanent and necessary impulse which it recognises can never be entirely lived and should perhaps not be attempted. In a truer and more penetrating sense than the phrase usually implies, this novel is a 'poem *in* prose'. It is not, that is to say, written in a 'poetic' prose. Rather the poetic affirmation of romance is set within a prose which refuses ever quite to assimilate it. As with *Chronicle*, the meaning of the work lies in the tension between its 'poetry' and its 'prose'. I say tension because in refusing quite to assimilate the romance it also protects it.

With a happy insight which encompasses the popular note of the book, Michael Wood has expressed something of this double effect by referring to this novel as Márquez' 'bolero'.[10] In his early journalism, both while he was still based on the Caribbean coast and when suddenly removed to Bogotá, a city incidentally whose name is actively avoided in the novel, Márquez often wrote warmly of the popular song tradition of the coastal region. Wood's formula catches very well the positive spirit of Márquez' popular expression of the romantic impulse. But there is a body of musical allusion in the text of the novel itself which reinforces the literary historical allusions and gives his populism a challenging edge.

I have already indicated the significance of soap opera but more importantly there are many references in the novel to the characters' love of music and especially of opera proper. Music, for example, is supremely important to Doctor Urbino and he raises the topic early in his courtship of Fermina:

'Le gusta la música?'
Lo preguntó con una sonrisa encantadora, de un modo casual, pero ella no le correspondió.
'A qué viene la pregunta?' preguntó a su vez.
'La música es importante para la salud.' dijo el.
Lo creía de veras, y ella iba a saber muy pronto y por el resto de su vida que el tema de la música era casi una fórmula mágica que el usaba para proponer una amistad, pero en aquella momento lo interpretó como una burla. (p. 178)

'Do you like music?'
'Why do you ask?' she asked in turn.
'Music is important for health,' he said.
He really believed this, and she was to know very soon, and for the rest of her life, that the subject of music was almost a magic formula that he used to propose friendship, but at that moment she took it for a joke. (p. 122)

Through Dr Urbino, Márquez introduces music as a touchstone in the book at large. Music seems to be a sustaining power of life itself even for this man whose profession is medicine. Fermina soon sympathises with this. She regularly accompanies him to the opera and the opening of *Les Contes d'Hoffmann* is one of their supreme joint memories of their honeymoon in Europe. Nonetheless, the unequal note of this opening is maintained in that the primary enthusiasm is always his. And there is a similar pattern of inequality with respect to Florentino. The great musical enthusiast in his life is his uncle, Leo XII, with 'su afición maniática por el *bel canto*' (p. 384) / 'his maniacal love of bel canto' (p. 268). Florentino sympathises with, rather than actually participates in, this taste. Hence 'se conmovió' (p. 391) / 'he was moved' (p. 272) when his uncle sang *addio alla vita* from *Tosca* to celebrate Florentino's assuming the presidency of the river boat company but he would not think to join in.

The musical references point to a realm or value that largely escapes verbal expression. This stands partly in ludicrous contrast to reality, as when uncle Leo, as a would-be Dionysus, loses his false teeth trying to impose the power of music on the creatures of the jungle. Yet it is also partly transformative as in the early incident of the concert in which Dr Urbino, having been scandalised by the revelation of his dead friend's long-standing mistress, is brought to show 'lealtad con la mujer que había repudiado cinco horas antes,'

(p. 65) / 'loyalty to the woman he had repudiated five hours earlier' (p. 42). His change of heart is effected more by the influence of music than by the intercession of his wife. The whole episode of the concert plays on the interweaving of the music with the emotional and social reality of the occasion.

Music appears throughout the book as the ambivalent but indispensable power of romance. And since opera in particular is both a musical and a dramatic genre, it is obliged to spell out formally its remove from realist terms and in doing so it speaks for the novel too. What an opera might express, the novel vindicates and protects. The doubleness is embodied in the different kinds, and degrees, of musical appreciation seen in the characters. It is evident that Dr Urbino, the connoisseur and promoter of opera, has a rational and sublimative relation to it, while Florentino's uncle, in keeping with the more romantic tenor of his life, actually sings. By contrast, Fermina and Florentino are sympathetically associated with music and opera without being enthusiasts or direct participants. This is because they ultimately wish to live out its values in reality. To make it possible for them to do so, the novel adjusts its own imaginative lens, its implicit contract with the reader, by means of the opera theme.

This can be seen by the exercise of imagining a passage of Márquez verbally unchanged but understood in a Flaubertian spirit. Borges' Pierre Menard would have us read the text of *Don Quixote* to yield a modern, non-Cervantean meaning.[11] That was a difficult feat which even Menard failed to achieve. But it is relatively easy to imagine the following passage as written by Flaubert:

La temporada se abrió con una compañía francesa de ópera cuya novedad era un arpa en la orquesta, y cuya gloria inolvidable era la voz inmaculada y el talento dramático de una soprano turca que cantaba descalza y con anillos de pedrerías preciosas en los dedos de los pies. A partir del primer acto apenas si se veía el escenario y los cantantes perdieron la voz por el humo de las tantas lámparas de aceite de corozo, pero los cronistas de la ciudad se cuidaron muy bien de borrar estos obstáculos menudos y de magnificar los memorables. Fue sin duda la iniciativa más contagiosa del doctor Urbino, pues la fiebre de la ópera contaminó hasta los sectores menos pensados de la ciudad, y dio origen a toda una generación de Isoldas y Otelos, y Aidas y Sigfridos. (pp. 73–4)

The season opened with a French opera company whose novelty was a harp in the orchestra and whose unforgettable glory was the impeccable voice and dramatic talent of a Turkish soprano who sang barefoot and wore rings set with precious stones on her toes. After the first act the stage was hardly to be seen and the singers lost their voices because of the smoke from so many palm oil lamps, but the chroniclers of the city took care to erase these minor obstacles and to magnify what was memorable. Without a doubt it was Dr Urbino's most contagious initiative, for opera fever infected the most unexpected sections of the city and gave birth to a whole generation of Isoldes and Otellos and Aidas and Siegfrieds. (p. 48)

Márquez' vision here is no less ironical than Flaubert's would have been, but with a different kind of irony. In Flaubert, for example, we would know how to read the 'impeccable' voice of the Turkish soprano but in Márquez we cannot be so sure. If the 'chroniclers of the city' are adjusting their verbal lenses so, in his own way, is Márquez. Like Dr Urbino looking on the life of the same city, he loves it enough 'para verla con los ojos de la verdad' (p. 167) / 'to see it with the eyes of truth' (p. 115). Where a classic English novelist, like George Eliot, would say you can *only* see the human truth *when* looking with the eyes of love, Márquez is somewhere between that stance and the Flaubertian. And, once again, the final imagery of disease in the passage links this ambivalent complex of feeling to both the central motifs of cholera and romance. Dr Urbino, the rational and effective campaigner against the cholera, has himself been responsible for this 'contagious initiative'.

The fact that we can so readily perform the imaginary exercise of reading the passage in the spirit of Flaubert arises partly from the fact that opera has been a recurrent motif by which both realist and modernist writers have defined their own generic forms. In *Madame Bovary* itself, Emma's readiness to be emotionally caught up by a performance of *Lucia di Lammermoor* is treated with crushing irony. On the other hand, Joyce's *Ulysses*, and several consciously modernist works of Thomas Mann, not only present operatic experience in a more positive light, they use it as a partial model, or criterion, for their own conscious departures from realist form.

As a reading of Joyce, and of *Cholera* itself, reminds us, opera at the turn of the century was a highly popular form; and hence the desire of some of these earlier writers to distance themselves from it. It is significant that opera has acquired a new popularity, and a new kind of popularity, precisely over the period of Márquez' career for the late twentieth-century popularity of opera has been part of a transformation in the understanding of the form itself. That it now regularly attracts great theatrical directors reflects a more serious and integral understanding of its nature as musical drama. In the early 1960s it was possible to think of the middle part of the nineteenth century as a relatively weak period for drama. This judgement may indeed be a fair one but in making it one would now have to recognise that opera was one of the forms into which the dramatic imagination of the period went. And it could strike important notes of political feeling as was recognized by the crowds who drew Verdi's hearse through the streets singing the Israelites' chorus from *Nabucco*. That is why Márquez' late twentieth-century novel, set around the turn of the century, is able to unite in its operatic theme both the popular note of the earlier period and the generic appreciation of recent decades. A way of expressing the reservation about *Chronicle* would be to say that its love theme seemed to require the insertion of a different mode of fiction which it could only with tact and difficulty contain. As Márquez pulls out the stops for the return of Bayardo with his bag of unopened letters we might think of this, with some ironic intent, as his letter aria. In *Cholera*, by contrast, the whole work is made generically and consciously of a piece with its affirmation of romance. In a larger way, the whole literary movement of which Márquez is a part may be associated with the renewed, sophisticated appreciation of opera.

It is also no accident perhaps that the 'operatic' moment in *Chronicle* should have involved Angela's letters. For the letters which played a subordinate role in the earlier work have become a dominant motif, and narrative means, in the later one. Angela's letters were her means of expressing an emotional truth for which there was no other outlet. A comparable use of a letter occurs with the death of Dr Urbino's father, Dr Marco Aurelio Urbino. This imposing public figure is not really known even to his own family until they read his posthumous letter 'de amor febril' (p. 170) / 'of feverish love' (p. 116) written to them on his death bed. This letter shows his given name to be indeed an appropriate one yet 'nunca antes de esa carta se le había mostrado tal como era en cuerpo y alma, por pura y simple timidez' (pp. 170–1) / 'before this letter he had never revealed himself body and soul out of pure and simple shyness' (p. 117).

But the letters of Florentino are a central narrative device defining the emotional ambivalence, and the fictional bracketing, of the romantic experience. They are a way of balancing and interrelating the kinds of truth and falsehood in romance. His early letters, along with Fermina's subsequent rejection of him, suggest the dangers of delusion. Yet in the longer term the impulse of these letters is vindicated when he finds a newly realistic mode of expression. He has to learn that the bubble of romance bursts when its truth is too crudely counted on, or literalised. Fermina is then so struck by the wisdom of these later letters, that she decides to keep them as a series and to think of them as a book. If this is a hint towards the traditional device of the correspondence which becomes the book we are reading, then it is a reminder of the partial origin of modern realist fiction in the epistolary novel of the eighteenth century.

In the eighteenth century, this device was usually a way of exploring levels of sincerity in the character's self-presentation while keeping the whole form within that 'air of reality' which Henry James was to see as the hallmark of the novel tradition as he inherited it. There was a close homology between the narrative literalism of such fiction and the literalistic understanding of the ethics of sentiment in the same period.[12] If Márquez returns to some such value in the letter as mediating between the narrative form and the emotional ethic of the book, it is not by using the letters themselves as the narrative medium. The letters are always firmly placed within his own third-person narrative frame. Coming at the other end of the realist tradition, Márquez needs to use the letters not to reinforce the reality effect of his own narrative but to provide protective enclaves *from* such an effect. Only through that route does he then provide an implicit model for the ultimate meaning of his own story. Like both the opera and Florentino's letters, the novel creates a privileged but necessary space.

In sum, this novel vindicates its vision of romantic love through a constant, glancing texture of literary and cultural allusion. Yet the ultimately important emphasis has to be that, in keeping with Márquez' fundamental populism, these allusions never become too self-conscious, or detached from the narrative subject. The novel can be read innocently without being misread. The apparent casualness of the narrative is important, not just as a concealment of art: it is an aspect of the vision. The narrative bravura is part of the point. Henry James, D. H. Lawrence and Ivan Turgenev, while seeing the power of Flaubert, all saw something ultimately stultifying in the resolute imposition of his artistic will. For James and Turgenev particularly, we might say that the tragic vision of Flaubert was only indirectly revealed in his works and was most truly and fully embodied in the Sisyphean artistry these works imply. Flaubert himself was the true tragic hero of his *œuvre*. By contrast, while showing a complete narrative mastery, Márquez creates the maximum open endedness both of tone and of narrative resolution. The necessity and impossibility of romance are embodied in the teasing, flirtatious quality of the story-telling. Whereas the early fiction frequently had a sub-textual self-consciousness, this late work in particular puts its fictional play on the surface.

The critical danger, in seeking to make these effects explicit, is of breaking the butterfly upon a wheel. The glancingness is all. It may be helpful as a final emphasis, therefore, to give some examples of moments in which the playfully open-ended spirit of narrative self-consciousness in the work leaves the reader wondering how much to read into it at any given moment. The general spirit of the work creates a constant flicker of possibility, a kind of spray where the surface of its medium meets ours, such that one cannot be sure whether one has actually been splashed or has just imagined it. The meaning seems to lie more in the possibility than in the specific interpretation.

Are we, for example, to see a formal joke in the following incident which has little necessity from a purely narrative point of view?

Alguna vez probo apenas una tisana de manzanilla, y la devolvió con una sola frase: 'Esta vaina sabe a ventana.' Tanto ella como las criadas se sorprendieron, porque nadie sabía de alguien que hubiera bebido una ventana hervida, pero cuando probaron la tisana tratando de entender, entendieron: sabía a ventana. (p. 324)

Once he barely tasted some chamomile tea and returned it, with the single remark: 'This stuff tastes of window.' She and the servants were equally surprised because nobody had ever heard of anyone drinking boiled window, yet when they tried the tea in an effort to understand, they understood; it tasted of window. (pp. 226–7)

The reader here is in the same position as Fermina and the servants except that they can actually resolve the matter by tasting the tea. Fiction, like language itself, requires a consensual acceptance of external reality although fiction is also the pre-eminent medium through which the boundaries of consensus can be explored and renegotiated. At the level of language Dr Urbino's remark seems almost surrealist yet at the level of the fictional reality it turns out to have an accurately referential truth. Since we cannot taste the tea for ourselves, the remark retains for us its flickering ambiguity. It is strictly a play with the order of discourse itself, yet it is the more playful in being barely emergent from the order of the subject-matter. Behind the joke about the tea lies Dr Urbino's objection when food is not prepared with love. As was remarked in the preceding chapter, John Bayley would make this a fundamental principle of literary creation.

Or again, Florentino seems to incorporate a metafictional wit in the episode with the mirror. On one occasion during his fifty-year wait, he gets to see Fermina for several hours from fairly close up by the lucky placing of a mirror in a restaurant. He subsequently buys the mirror although its antique frame costs him dear. He is not interested in the frame but simply in the mirror which has contained the image of the beloved. Florentino is expressing his romantic extravagance by reversing the traditional image of realist vision. Once again, the episode is carried by its charm and can undoubtedly be read without such literary historical associations but part of its underlying toughness lies in its carrying the challenge into the enemy's territory. After all, even when used as a metaphor of realism, the image in the mirror is strictly a virtual one. The function of fiction at any time is not passive. It does not merely reflect but makes *us* reflect, and all reality is in some sense chosen.

The lightness of touch bears equally on the running comparison with Flaubert. Márquez is not necessarily placing *Cholera* on a footing with *Madame Bovary*. Indeed, the tact of the novel lies in its nice judgement of its own relative weight. Nor is it a question of displacing Flaubert's vision, as if proving it 'wrong'. Works of fictional imagination don't stand in that sort of relation to each other. It is rather a matter of taking a classic metaphysical vision, as incorporated in an equally classic formal mode, and using this to define a contrary one.

In fact, the danger here would be of allowing the order of allusion to take over too much so that the book becomes merely parasitical on an earlier one. There is a recognisable late twentieth-century fictional sub-genre of the rewritten classic. Jean Rhys's *Wide Sargasso Sea* (1966) is the most distinguished example, and *Flaubert's Parrot* a close runner-up. Márquez' allusiveness, however, steers well clear of this. His vision is there very much in its own right while using allusion, humorously and parenthetically, to define and place itself.

However, if this novel ends with his central characters challenging their social world and the very conditions of existence by their final, and as it were eternal, trip on the Magdalena river, this points towards the different world of Márquez' next novel, in which the weightiness of the historical subject could hardly be more ambitious.

8

Solitude and Solidarity:
The General in his Labyrinth

Márquez' last novel to date is quite different again from all its predecessors. In some respects it is his most ambitious in that it imagines the last months in the life of a world historical figure, Simón Bolívar. Bolívar's achievement was to gain independence for the Spanish colonies in the northern half of the South American continent but his true ambition had been greater: it was to create a unified state out of all the Spanish colonies and thereby give them a collective power comparable to that of the USA and the major European states. When he died, prematurely aged, at forty-eight, it was already clear that this larger ambition was not going to be realised. Local and national jealousies were more powerful than the longer-term regional commonality of political interest, culture and historical experience. Whereas his contemporary, Napoleon Bonaparte, had had a heroic career followed by a public defeat and imposed isolation, Bolívar's life, on this reading, was more ambiguously a defeat perceived, in solitude, within an apparent victory. He suffers, or withdraws into, a more mysterious isolation.

In the last months of his life, which are less well documented historically, Bolívar sailed down the Magdalena river from near Bogatá to the coast. His stated intention of leaving the country altogether may not have represented the whole truth. Márquez depicts him as partly taking advantage of the delay in obtaining a passport and thus getting drawn into one last attempt at unification by supporting a military coup. But for the most part his enforced inactivity, and his declining health, make it natural that the narrative should consist of a stock-taking of his past life. As with *Cholera* and *No One Writes*, the narrative is something of a *tour de force* in consciously filling the

127

time.

An intimate portrait of acknowledged greatness is always an artistic risk. The classic historical novelists, such as Scott and Stendhal, chose more average characters to bear the principal weight of their narratives. Major figures in history are best given a minor role in a novel, for it is hard to avoid either a false aura of grandeur or else an effect, whether deliberately or not, of debunking. Or else the figure may be co-opted to a viewpoint of easy historical hindsight. Márquez is clearly aware of all these dangers and it is a testimony to his skill and experience that he has been able to carry off the occasion. Or at least, I believe he has. Other readers are less sure. Philip Swanson has remarked on the relative flatness of this book after the brilliance of earlier novels.[1] This is an important observation and in offering a rationale for the book I wish to accommodate and explain this quality rather than deny it. I believe the book has a peculiar poignancy when seen as a stock-taking on Marquez' part as well as Bolivar's.

If *The General* is radically different from all the novels discussed so far it is perhaps most importantly so in reversing the narrative premises of *Hundred Years*. I have already remarked that *Chronicle* inverts *Hundred Years* by placing the fiction within the chronicle rather than the chronicle within the fiction. But *The General* is more radical again.

First, of course, *Chronicle* does not have the mythic ambition, or the sweep of historical vision, attempted by both these other works. But *The General* 'answers' *Hundred Years* on a comparable plane of historical vision and in doing so it once again changes and amplifies the meaning of the Buendía story. Melquíades' foretold chronicle of the Buendías encloses them within an historical cycle. Yet the comic tone of the book itself seems to elude the darkness of this destiny just as Gabriel escapes to Paris. In a sense, it is as if the story of the Buendías, however tragically representative, is being firmly consigned to the past. That is where they are felt to belong. In this respect, *The General* does the opposite. It takes a real historical figure, whose life's ambition seems to have been a failure now permanently inscribed in history, but it sees this figure as having a potential impact even in the historical present. Bolívar is always looking over the head of his own immediate situation to a longer historical vision which makes him at times the contemporary of the reader rather than of the other characters. This could, of course, be merely a cheap trick of historical hindsight but in the present case it is rather a way of focusing the continuing but problematic pertinence of Bolívar's ambition. The ambition, that is to say, is just as needful, and just as Quixotic, in our own day. Although the life of an individual is unrepeatable, in the life of a community history may indeed give second opportunities. The failed ambition of Bolívar is still relevant to a full liberation of the region.

There are therefore several moments when Bolívar looks forward with a prophetic eye:

> Sus motivos, como de costumbre, tenían un aliento profético: mañana, cuando él no estuviera, el proprio gobierno que ahora pedía apoyar haría venir a Santander, y éste regresaría coronado de gloria a liquidar los escombros de sus sueños, la patria inmensa y única que él había forjado en tantos años de guerras y sacrificios sucumbiría en pedazos, les partidos se descuartizarían entre sí, su nombre sería vituperado y su obra pervertida en la memoria de los siglos.[2]

> His arguments, as usual, had a touch of the prophetic: tomorrow, when he was no longer there, the very government which now sought his support would bring back Santander, and Santander would come, crowned with glory, to destroy the remains of his dreams, the immense and unique country which he had created through so many years of war and sacrifice would collapse in pieces, the parties would dismember each other, while his own name would be defamed and his life's work perverted in the memory of coming centuries.[3]

There is double effect in this. The long, spiralling sentence, not quite the general's or the narrator's, blends historical hindsight with a melancholy fatalism which we can see as partly the general's depressed mood rather than simply Márquez' analysis. It is not true, for example, that Bolívar would simply be defamed, he would rather perhaps be co-opted as heroic legend, yet his substantial fears were to prove justified. In this way, we sense the interaction of a genuinely large-scale vision and its attendant temptations, in this case of fatalism. Yet the temptation in our own day, and perhaps even increased with the 'advantage' of hindsight, is still that of fatalism, a sense of being overwhelmed by historical process or political minutiae. Nietzsche pointed out the subtle inextricability of the uses and disadvantages of the historical sense.[4] A sense of history can impede the very actions it informs and motivates.

What Márquez finds in Bolívar's 'obra', the normal term for a work of art, is an historical vehicle for his own modern vision of regional solidarity. It is a vehicle that can simultaneously weigh the force of those pressures that will always stand against this vision. The important thing, then or now, is not to lose the larger vision for it is this which gives meaning to the immediate foreground of politics. And so Bolívar says of Santander:

'La verdadera causa fue que Santander no pudo asimilar nunca la idea de que este continente fuera un solo país,' dijo el general. 'La unidad de América le quedaba grande.' (p. 125)

'The real reason was that Santander could never take in the idea of this continent as a single country,' said the general. 'The unity of America was too big for him.' (p. 117)

The fictional 'obra' of Márquez echoes the equally ideal 'obra' of Bolívar. The fragile idealism of a vision not realised in history remains as a kind of fiction to be known appropriately enough by means of the very fiction we are reading. The fact that it was a failed vision is what gives Márquez' fiction its sombre power and its political point. Yet Bolívar, of course, did leave his mark on history. He is a mythic hero in a truer, if less obvious, sense than with traditionally archetypal figures. Rather than a timeless value beyond particular historical occasions, he represents, on a grand scale, the workings of visionary purpose in history at all times. The interrelations of fictional imagination and historical record in the narrative suggest the inextricable interplay of vision and process in the making of history. This leads to the more radical difference from earlier works and explains why the relative flatness of the work may be deliberate and appropriate. If the patriarch was a 'magical realist' of sorts, the General is a specialist in disillusion.

Márquez is now taking for his narrative frame a real historical figure. Previously, he had presented fictions with equivocal, Cervantean framings of fictitious chronicle. His fiction had constantly played at being history. But now some of these same equivocations take on an opposite meaning as his fictional narrative of Bolívar's private thoughts constantly dissolves into the known history of the legendary figure. Whereas the 'mythical' and 'historical' framings of *Hundred Years* were teasingly superimposed, and remained teasing because they were constantly distinguished as categories, in *The General* the mythic and historical are merged. Yet even as they are merged in the narrative, the categorial distinction remains sufficiently alive in the reader's mind to read this merging as an awareness of the mythic texture of history itself. History is malleable to human purposes but these purposes are themselves mixed, contradictory and obscure. One way of understanding myth, in a modern context, is as the affirmation of collective purpose. Márquez is retrospectively affirming such a collective purpose as embodied in the figure of Bolívar just as W. B. Yeats, despite all his reservations about the Irish nationalist cause, had acknowledged such a collective significance in the events of 'Easter 1916'.[5] Yeats' poem is the classic expression of the inescapably mythic nature of history, both in the making and in what Nietzsche called the 'use' of it. It is this sense of apparently dispelling myth which explains the deliberate flatness of the narrative. But the dispelling is, of course, only apparent. Yeats was never more truly mythopoeic than when he claimed to be discarding myth and the same is true of Márquez in his presentation of Bolívar. The relative prosaicness, and it is only relative, is a feint like Yeats' claim that 'there is more enterprise in walking naked' or that the 'circus animals' had deserted him.[6]

Even so, the relative flatness of the book, if it is that, is not removed simply by seeing it as deliberate. If the narrative medium is successful it is offering something more subtly positive than this. And indeed I believe there is something more involved in the success of the book than Márquez' general maturity as a novelist. When the book was first announced its title suggested a possible parody of Latin American fiction through its central clichés. Any parodic implication is quickly dispelled on reading, but a subtler and more serious note of self-reference lurks in the text and is perhaps signalled by the title.

I have already remarked that, particularly in all the works since *Hundred Years*, there is an evident reworking of themes from earlier novels. Each novel exerts a questioning impact on one or more of its predecessors. *The General* is in keeping with this but with a different emphasis: it seems rather to depend on a summative assimilation of figures and motifs from several early works as if they might now be seen rather as its necessary precursors. Just as *Hundred Years* seemed to sum up an earlier phase of his fiction, so *The General* sums up the later phase with *Hundred Years* being once again the cardinal point of reference. It is as if Márquez' own previous *œuvre*, including the regionally representative *Hundred Years*, is being subtly invoked within the text so as to give the Bolívar figure a further dimension. His mythic historical significance is felt partly through invoking the summative weight of Márquez' earlier fiction.

The mythic figure of Bolívar, at once tangible yet ungraspable, seems an amalgam of earlier figures. This is not a matter of conscious allusion. Indeed, it is not so much specific figures as a weight of world view which is invoked. Márquez' refusal to wear his artistry upon his sleeve makes it peculiarly useful to highlight the constituents of that artistry by following what may indeed have been, at least in part and however consciously, his own creative route. The book, of course, stands quite sufficiently of itself. But readers of earlier Márquez cannot but note the recurrence of phrases and motifs which once had different meanings so that the ghosts of these earlier meanings constantly haunt the text, giving it an ambiguous penumbra of further suggestion.

For example, Márquez uses the 'había de' (was to) formula which had been a stylistic trade mark of *Hundred Years*. In the earlier novel this phrasing caught, from the very opening sentence, the sense of fatedness which hangs over the Buendías. Of course, this sense of fate was in no simple way borne out by the narrative. But the point is that the narrative framings and self-consciousness of the Buendías' story gave an extraordinary pregnancy to this simple, but formulaic, phrase. It is therefore with something of an ironic shock, like going to tread on a step which is not there, that the reader continues to encounter this phrase in *The General*. For one has learned to read it as freighted with destiny only to have constantly to recognise that in this new context it is recording simple historical facts taking place after the narrative present:

Soledad tenía el nombre bien puesto: cuatro calles de casas de pobres, ardientes y desoladas, a unas dos leguas de la antigua Barranca de San Nicolás, que en pocos años había de convertise en la ciudad más próspera y hospitalaria del país. (p. 215)

Soledad was well named: four streets of poor houses, burning and desolate, some two leagues from the former Barranca de San Nicolas, which in a few years was to turn itself into the most prosperous and hospitable city in the country. (p. 211)

The almost crassly obvious gift of 'history' to the novelist that one of Bolívar's last resting places should be called Soledad (solitude) is, tactfully, not exploited. It remains a fact of history just brought into parenthetic focus by the fictional lens. And so, too, the immediate future of the nearby town is recorded as an indifferent fact of history. That it should have been a prosperous future only reinforces the indifference. The failure of Bolívar's ideal was apparently not felt as a disaster. In this way, the 'había de' formula in this book has a bleaker melancholy about it as it is shorn of the pregnancy, albeit the sinister pregnancy, of its former use. As Borges pointed out, there can be comfort and importance in believing yourself to be specially fated.[7] But in *The General* that kind of mythic, or pseudo-mythic, comfort is made to fade into the common light of day. Mythic import is something that must be actively won from history. This makes for a flatter kind of narrative medium as suits the bleaker view of life. But it is also more bracing and forward-looking recognition. The implicit critique of the Buendías in *Hundred Years*, which has sometimes been overlooked, becomes the central recognition of *The General*.

It should also be noted that the reference to the Barranca de San Nicolás is entirely irrelevant to the ostensible theme of the novel. But this was to become the town of Barranquilla in which Marquez' own literary career started. Just as he avoids the modern name of Bogotá so he obliquely suggests the modern name of Barranquilla. The casualness of the personal allusion here makes it difficult to determine whether the general reader is supposed to notice it or not, although it is there and serves no other purpose. It precisely epitomises the way in which Bolivar's story is made to carry its charge into the present through the resonances of Marquez' reflection of his own *œuvre* while at the same time avoiding any overt or personal intrusion into the historical subject. Marquez manages to be meaningfully present and tactfully absent.

The apparently transparent narrative of *The General*, in other words, has a weight of implicit meditation within, or behind, it. In effect, our way of understanding Bolívar's largely unspoken ruminations behind his occasional summary comments is through the way this book recapitulates Márquez' own extended meditation on related themes throughout his previous career. We do not see in Bolívar an intellectual complexity of historical analysis so much as a shifting complexity of experience which could not be expressed as an idea. At the level of idea it seems simple because the function of the 'idea' in Bolívar's life has indeed been as a yardstick or sea-mark against the shifting tides of events and personalities. Márquez' own 'obra' has also been a many-sided meditation around the constant themes of solitude and solidarity which have come to a culmination in the figure of Bolívar.

Solitude and solidarity have been the dialectical poles of Márquez' thinking on both the personal and the political planes. The terms are variously opposed, mutually dependent and, at times, overlapping. The profound solitude of Bolívar is inseparable from his vision of regional solidarity. His mythic or legendary force even in his own day requires a constant reserve in all his ordinary human relations and he thinks of himself ultimately in historical rather than personal terms. But although his situation is special, psychologically Bolívar unites within himself several of Márquez' previous solitaries so that they contribute to our understanding of him as he in turn modifies our view of them. The most important of these, without forgetting the Patriarch, are the colonel and the doctor from *Leaf Storm*, the colonel from *No One Writes*, Colonel Aureliano Buendía, and Florentino Ariza. The figure of Bolívar is a reminder of all these figures from Márquez' earliest novella to his most recent novel.

At the beginning of his journey Bolívar is obliged to leave Santa Fe (Bogotá) as if he were an escaping bandit although only months before he had been given a spontaneous hero's welcome by the same population:

Nadie hubiera creído que el fuera el mismo de entonces, ni que fuera la misma aquella ciudad taciturna que abandonaba para siempre con precauciones de forajido. En ninguna parte se había sentido tan forastero como en aquellas callecitas yertas con casas iguales de tejados pardos y jardines íntimos con flores de buen olor, donde se cocinaba a fuego lento una comunidad aldeana, cuyas maneras relamidas y cuyo dialecto ladino servían más para ocultar que para decir. (General p. 48)

No one would have believed he was the same man as before, nor that it could be the same city, now silent, which he was leaving forever with the stealth of an outlaw. Nowhere had he felt such an outsider as in these tight little streets of houses, all alike with their brown roofs and private gardens of sweet smelling flowers, where the village community cooked on a slow fire and where the affected, cunning dialect served more to obscure thought than to speak it. (p. 40)

Márquez' personal distaste for Bogotá here focuses Bolívar's more general sense of being an outsider. The Spanish terms 'forajido' and 'forastero' seem to echo each other as in the English 'outlaw' and 'outsider'. It is as if being an outsider may in itself be somehow a crime against the community, or as if it arises as a punishment from the obscure, half-recognition of such a crime. Bolívar excites a nervousness in others such that his very bed-linen, as he discovers, is burned by his landlady. Like Florentino, he seems a carrier of the plague. At the same time his cut hair is kept by a woman who sees him, just as inhumanly perhaps, as a saint. Is this an opposite response or essentially the same? The bottomless ambivalence of solitude is a well from which Márquez continues to draw.

Bolívar's solitude is a conscious necessity on his part but it is no less of a personal burden for that. When advising the young Mexican, Iturbide, to return to his native country he says: 'Se sentirá forastero en todas partes, y eso es peor que estar muerte' (p. 228) / 'You will feel a stranger everywhere, and that is worse than being dead' (p. 224). The general's phrasing here conveys death as an active state and readers will remember from earlier works the folkloric interplay of death and solitude whereby these states were living gradations of each other. To be a mythic figure it may be necessary to be dead, even in your own lifetime.

The world-historical and legendary significance of Bolívar raises the solitude theme to a new power and makes it less of a personal or psychological question. Yet in being so it echoes significances already evident in earlier figures where it had seemed more simply personal or where its ambivalences had remained obscure. Mario Vargas Llosa has commented well on the peculiar effect for the colonel in *No One Writes* when he finally walks home with his fighting cock through the cheering crowd of townspeople. As Vargas Llosa says, we know they are supporting him yet we feel their essential remoteness for him as if they were in fact a hostile crowd. The very expression of their solidarity only reinforces the sense of his solitude. At this moment, the two contrasting experiences of Bolívar's welcome to Santa Fe de Bogotá and the manner of his leaving are merged for the colonel. A similar ambivalence was approached from the other end in *Leaf Storm* as that earlier colonel, through an act of solidarity with the outsider figure of the doctor, had to face the hostility of the town. But that was within a more rationally discriminated situation. With the colonel of *No One Writes* it runs counter to expectation and points to some deeper, more intrinsic, source of his solitude.

In this respect, Bolívar, as a literary character, is an avatar of that obscure colonel. Like the colonel, he is filling time, after a lifetime of duty, in the distant and threatening shadow of national politics. Their stories both take place through the same difficult season from October to December. Both are at the mercy of their guts, whose condition is explicitly imaged in Bolívar's case as a 'desobediencia del cuerpo' (p. 237) /'disobedience of the body' (p. 235). Both consume 'mazomorro'/'maize mush'. Both wait anxiously for the post. And, most importantly, both assert their values with a Quixotic conviction which obliges others to play along with it:

> Sin embargo, tuvieron que continuar toda la noche oyéndolo anunciar en tono profético cómo iban a reconstituir desde sus orígenes y esta vez para siempre el vasto imperio de sus ilusiones. Montilla fue el único que se atrevió a contrariar el stupor de quienes creyeron estar escuchando los desafueros de un loco. (p. 257)

> Nonetheless, they had to listen to him the whole night propounding in a prophetic tone how they were going to recreate from the beginning, and this time for ever, the vast empire of his illusions. Montilla was the only one who dared to challenge the stupor of those who believed they were listening to the ravings of a madman. (p. 256)

The Quixotry of the Colonel was explicit; the eventual hopelessness of his ideal was always evident. In the present passage, the references to 'illusions' and 'ravings' are encircled with ambiguity, since Montilla goes on to remind the company of a former occasion on which Bolívar's similarly absurd prophecy had been justified. In Don Quixote's case his madness was cured, or his illusion was destroyed, by those who pretended to go along with it. But here, such bystanders are themselves seen to be in a state of stupor in making such a judgement. Márquez expresses the inevitability of this judgement in the immediate situation while leaving open the question of its ultimate validity. Once again, their apparent solidarity, their not wishing to challenge the General, throws his solitary conviction into relief. Like Melquíades in his solitary room, the General expresses a truth which no one, apart from the odd initiate, can begin to understand. In this case, not because of its obscurity but because of its grandeur. A kernel of truth is protected by the solitude of incomprehension and in that respect the colonel's laconic obduracy lives again in the visionary concentration of Márquez' Bolívar.

If the spirit of the colonel lives on transformed in the General, the same may more clearly be said with respect to Colonel Aureliano Buendía. On the face of it, the Buendías were given to psychic somnambulism and a lack of historical sense after the insomnia sickness, while Bolívar is just the opposite. His present nights of insomnia arise from his ceaseless meditation on the making of history. And whereas Col. Aureliano comes to see a hollow pride as his true motivation for fighting in the civil wars, there is no doubt of the seriousness and integrity of Bolívar's purpose. Yet in this very inversion we sense the affinity of a mirror image. Like Col. Aureliano, Bolívar orders the execution of a man he loves and respects. And although he draws no chalk circle around himself he has 'el halo mágico del poder' (p. 40) /'the magical halo of power' (p. 32) and his closest aides are always kept at a distance. The affinity is the more telling for the difference. What was revealed as a personal and family trait of Col. Aureliano is seen to be the necessary condition of Bolívar's historical role. Hence if we sense in him any actual echo of Aureliano it adds an ambivalence to each of them, and gives a further pathos and mystery to Bolívar. Is it only a similarity of circumstance or is there, of necessity, an Aureliano in Bolívar? The account of Bolivar's personal life suggests this may be so.

Col. Aureliano had discovered an essential emptiness and solitude not just in war but also in sex. The myriad anonymous loves of his military campaign years raised a theme that was developed rather differently in the love life of Florentino Ariza, which leads in turn to the love theme of *The General*. Whereas Col. Aureliano's affairs were brief and anonymous encounters in the dark, both Florentino and the General have appreciative and personal affairs with a succession of highly individual and impressive women. But Florentino's underlying love for Fermina means that all his other affairs are, just as much as the General's, subordinate to an ideal commitment.

In this regard, Florentino and the General, who sail into their respective eternities of fiction and myth on the Magdalena river, are opposite aspects of each other. Both understand that the supreme values of love and of history, as in *Antony and Cleopatra*, are ultimately incompatible, and each makes his fundamental choice. Bolívar, like Col. Aureliano, takes to his historical career after the death of his wife when they are both young. It is explicit that had she lived he would not have done so and his reaction is partly an attempt to stifle the grief. But history gave another gift to the novelist, and to Bolívar, in the figure of Manuela Saenz. This much younger woman, with her remarkable spirit and intelligence, was his lover for the last eight years of his life. Life does not throw up many such and she provides the test case for the General's ultimate commitments and personal character.

But the issue she focuses is a broader one. The General, for example, is shocked to learn that a former associate, Joaquín Mosquera, has passed nearby without visiting him and has been criticising him to others. Indeed, Mosquera's final summative remark echoes, and inverts, Bolívar's first utterance on the opening page of the novel:

'Recuérdenlo bien' les dijo. 'Ese tipo no quiere a nadie.'

José Palacios sabía cuán sensible era el general a semejante reproche. Nada le dolía tanto, ni lo ofuscaba tanto como que alguien pusiera en duda sus afectos, y era capaz de apartar océanos y derriba montañas con su terrible poder de seducción, hasta convencerlo de su error. En la plenitud de la gloria, Delfina Guardiola, la bella de Angostura, le había cerrado en las narices las puertas de su casa, enfurecida por sus veleidades. 'Usted es un hombre eminente, general, más que ninguno,' le dijo. 'Pero el amor le queda grande.' Él se metió por la ventana de la cocina y permaneció con ella durante tres días, y no sólo estuvo a punto de perder una batalla, sino también el pellejo, hasta lograr que Delfina confiara en su corazón. (p. 221)

'Remember it well,' he told them, 'This fellow loves no one.'

José Palacios knew how sensitive the general was to a reproach like this. Nothing pained him, or bewildered him, so much as when someone doubted his affections and he was capable of parting the seas or moving mountains with his terrible power of seduction until he had convinced them of their error. At the height of his glory, Delfina Guardiola, the belle of Angostura, had closed her door in his face enraged by his fickleness. 'You are a great man, General, greater than anyone,' she said, 'but love is too big for you.' He got in through the kitchen window and stayed with her for three days, nearly losing not just a battle but his own skin, until she believed in his love. (p. 217)

Where Col. Aureliano comes to recognise his inability to love, the General puts the energy of a Don Juan into denying, or repressing, this recognition. Nonetheless, in his case we feel this charge, although true, to be in some sense unfair or beside the point. With him, it is more difficult to distinguish a personal failing from a necessity of the case. Manuela Saenz, who truly understands him, feels everything that Delfina does in this episode, yet she stands by him, and his cause, with total solidarity. The radical nature of his 'choice' is pointed up by the phrasing, as Delfina's remark on his inability to love echoes his own remark, quoted earlier, on Santander's inability to conceive the idea of regional unity. Such criticisms of the General seem pertinent while failing to encompass the whole truth. He remains judgementally out of reach.

The public nature of Bolívar's life, and its magnification in legend, make him, of course, a special case but it is also a way of placing in an unusually strong light Márquez' treatment of personal identity at all times. The memory of earlier figures in this book has a two-way effect. If the previous fiction prepares us for this one, so this late novel provides a new lens through which to read the earlier ones. The character of the General does not just echo some of his previous solitaries, it is an apotheosis of Márquez' characterisation generally. For alongside his critical emphasis on solitude there has been a consistent respect for the privacy of his characters.

Personal identity in Márquez is not a continuous self-creation from nothing as in the Sartrean conception, although it encompasses something of that lonely responsibility. Nor is it merely a play of external forces as in some versions of Marxist or naturalistic thinking. It is an inner region in which the 'external' is constantly transformed; a process which cannot be encompassed simply on the plane of critical self-consciousness which is privileged in both these other conceptions. That is why responsibility is, in the first instance, not to the world but to the self. You have first to have a meaningful self. This means maintaining both its necessary separateness and its internal integrity; its capacity to look inwards as well as outwards.

These interlinked recognitions were strongly figured in *Hundred Years* as the Buendías lost, in the insomnia sickness, their relationship to their night-time selves and Melquíades retired to tell their story in solitude. In the unvisited centre of the house, he became the expression of the unconscious self of the family which they were to experience externally as a fate. In other words, what was symbolically thematised in the narrative structure and magical texture of *Hundred Years* is Márquez' sense of personal identity as being at all times a mysterious wholeness which is to be actively respected but which cannot be consciously or more directly grasped. Melquíades may show the parchments, just as the unconscious may show your dreams, but both sources of wisdom remain incomprehensible and unregarded as long as they await translation into the language of day-time consciousness.

That is why Márquez always communicates a strong reserve about the inner forum of the self, both on his own behalf as author and on behalf of his characters. The opening of *The General* establishes the spirit of this:

> José Palacios, su servidor más antiguo, lo encontró flotando en las aguas depurativas de la bañera, desnudo y con los ojos abiertos, y creyó que se había ahogado. Sabía que ése era uno de sus muchos modos de meditar, pero el estado de éxtasis en que yacía a la deriva parecía de alguien que ya no era de esta mundo. No se atrevió a acercarse . . . (p. 11)

> José Palacios, his oldest servant, found him floating in the cleansing waters of the bath, naked and open-eyed, and thought he must have drowned. He knew that this was one of his many ways of meditating but the state of ecstasy in which he lay drifting was that of someone no longer of this world. He did not dare to approach . . . (p. 3)

Bolívar is first approached through his unapproachability but the apparently special case of Bolívar focuses a more general property of Márquez' presentation of character. We have already seen how he constantly withholds omniscience to preserve the mystery of the individual. Of course, his technique in this book of never actually naming Bolívar, while referring at one point to Bolivia, is in keeping with the subsequently mythic status of the figure. In 'Easter 1916' Yeats only named the executed patriots at the end when they had been transformed into figures of myth. As private individuals in the body of the poem they remained nameless. But Márquez' way of referring to Bolívar throughout as the General equally echoes his earlier method of referring to the colonel in *No One Writes*. Although the latter is not a world historical figure, Márquez accords him the same essential courtesy. The patrician reserve of the colonel, which is respected by his son's friends, is most significantly respected by the author himself.

The self resists theoretical understanding. It has often come to be seen therefore as an illusion when viewed in a highly theoretical light. Yet on the everyday political and personal planes the capacity to distinguish differing degrees of self-knowledge and responsibility remains meaningful and important. Márquez' characterisation reflects, and one might say respects, the necessary unknowability of the self, both to itself and to others. D. H. Lawrence used the image of the 'foreigner' to highlight the separateness and unknowability which are necessary to true relatedness. In his view, relationship is never a merging; it is only a relationship because the beings are distinct and should indeed, in a personal relationship, even be polar. True relationship is always a polar tension between unknowable entities. Something comparable is implied in Márquez. Where the tension beween difference and relationship collapses it is possible to fall into the abyss of solitude, as happens to the doctor in *Leaf Storm*. Or it is possible to become one of the herd like the townspeople in the same story. The former may be a greater suffering but the latter is the greater ignominy.

Márquez' strong sense of identity as a constant, responsible negotiation between an inner and outer is perhaps most strikingly figured in the presentation of speech throughout his fiction, and once again the figure of Bolívar throws a fresh light on its significance. Bolívar is keenly aware of himself as a public figure. His utterances are habitually deliberate and have a lapidary concentration. Márquez' possible artistic difficulty in according to Bolívar a speech adequate to the status of the figure yet without being unrealistic and stagey is met by placing the consciousness of this difficulty within Bolívar himself. With him, all utterance regains its etymological force as 'outering'. His speech repeatedly takes on the quality of pronouncements or aphorisms emerging in a highly self-conscious way from a constant, private process of reflection whose mystery is only partly illuminated by the utterances themselves. As his manservant, José Palacios, remarks, n a comparably lapidary manner: 'Lo que mi señor piensa, sólo mi señor lo sabe' (p. 184) / 'What my master thinks, only my master knows' (p. 178).

Yet we do not feel Bolívar, or Márquez on his behalf, to be straining for the historically resonant phrase. His letters are contrasted in this respect with Santander's. Bolívar, we are given to understand, writes to the moment and would have his letters destroyed, whereas Santander always writes with an eye to posterity. Santander's language exists, that is to say, only in the outer dimension whereas Bolívar's is the meeting point, and the point of tension, between inner and outer, present and future.

But a further reason for feeling Bolívar's carefully considered speech to be natural to him is that it is not essentially different from the relationship of speech to narrative in Márquez' fiction generally. In Márquez' fictional world it *is* natural. All Márquez' morally central characters have a tendency to this considered and lapidary speech set off by the narrative prose or by the less-considered speech of others. Again, the ending of *No One Writes* is exemplary. The colonel's final word, 'Mierda'/'Shit', is detached from his wife's question, which provokes it by a few lines of narrative. During these lines it ceases to be an immediate reply to her and becomes a multi-layered summative statement. These lines of narrative make us participate in the implied weight of reflection without foreclosing its ambivalence. We only have the one word that sums it up.

Most commonly, however, the process is simply implied, as it is for the colonel in the body of the preceding narrative. We do not see his process of reflection truly from the inside and very possibly there would be nothing, at that level, to 'see', for his consciousness might be a misleading index of his inner process. The relation of narrative to speech in Márquez constantly implies some such inchoate private process emerging suddenly into a public statement or decision. The two big decisions of Col. Aureliano, first to fight for the liberal cause and then later to give up, are both comprehensible and yet, especially when taken in conjunction, they retain a measure of the arbitrary and the impenetrable. Again, this is an especially striking rather than an unusual case. The well-springs of resilience, and the sources of such decisions, are rarely available to inspection even for the individual concerned.

In sum, while *The General* stands quite independently of the preceding works it is subtly modified when read as part of the *œuvre*. The figure of Bolívar is in some ways a lesser one than we may have expected. That is the disarming feint. But more subliminally he echoes a body of experience enshrined in a world view, itself shifting and internally modified, built up over all the preceding works. This gives a surprising resonance to what may be a deliberate or an intuitive flatness in the narrative. At the same time, the special stature of Bolívar leads us in turn to see his fictive precursors in a fresh light. If *Hundred Years* seemed for a time the summary and *terminus ad quem* of Márquez' earlier fiction, *The General* has a comparably strategic value in his career as a whole. Melquíades, as wise historian, and Bolívar, as great historical actor and visionary, are perhaps equally solitary. But in *The General* Márquez inverts the technique and meaning of *Hundred Years* to give his many previous solitaries an echo in the great dream of solidarity.

9

Conclusion

As one progresses through Márquez' *œuvre* its density of self-reference becomes increasingly evident. This is partly because the author, like any other author, has his particular preoccupations and language from which he inevitably creates a distinctive imaginative world. But I have resisted Vargas Llosa's emphasis on the 'deicidal' creation of a special fictional world since in Márquez the individual works conduct an implicit self-critical dialogue with each other and thereby resist totalisation. In fact the constant mutual adjustment between individual works is more marked after *Hundred Years* and there is a perceptible change in the kind of self-reference that occurs before and after that novel.

Many of the stories and novellas before *Hundred Years* share a common location: either a version of Macondo or the 'town' on the river. And some characters, such as the two priests, the 'Pup' and Father Angel, appear in several of these works. Hence the apparently summative force of *Hundred Years* as an imaginative mode was increased and naturalised by its placing so many of these events within an overall history. It is therefore understandable that the close interrelation of the early fictions at the level of character and event should have led to some rather literalistic arguments as critics discussed which of these works had the 'same' locations.[1]

But strictly speaking, these locations have been created within different imaginative worlds and are no more the same than the 'London' of *Little Dorrit* is the same as that of *Great Expectations*. The realism of *No One Writes* is in a slightly different register from the world that accommodates the mysterious lampoons of *In Evil Hour*. The self-reference of early Márquez seems pitched somewhere between the cumulative creation of a common fictional region, as in Faulkner, and a centrifugal impulse towards the creating of

144

different imaginative worlds. Up to and including the publication of *Hundred Years*, the more literalistic, Faulknerian commonality seemed the stronger principle and it would have been pedantic to insist otherwise. But the latter part of his *œuvre* has made it clear that the variety of imaginative premises is equally important although this itself, of course, can only be significant within a commonality of historical and thematic preoccupations. Only on some common ground could the works implicitly converse with each other, or have something to converse about.

Hence, despite the distinctive tone and 'world' of Márquez' fiction the internal echoing of his *œuvre* ultimately reflects a fundamental impersonality; a disappearance of the author at the level of personality or opinion. Each fiction creates its own meditative space so that its truth is absolute but only within its own sphere. Far from being the expression of personal opinion, his fiction actively resists this. The cumulative effect is to build a strong sense of a distinctive personal vision which is always elusively out of reach as a summative whole.

It is evident whenever Márquez discusses his own fiction, as in the occasional interview, that he exerts a careful control over what he will, and will not, say. This authorial reserve can be felt as a guiding spirit within the fiction and, just as significantly, he treats his characters with a similar respect for their privacy. He can, of course, be intimate with them. We follow the colonel of *No One Writes* into the privy. But it is precisely this which throws into relief the more essential sense of the colonel's inner being as one to which we are not being allowed access. The carefully curtailed omniscience enforces the character's inviolability.

This reserve underlies the way the speech of Márquez' central characters typically tends to the lapidary and the aphoristic. It is not a baring of the soul, or an elaboration of a view, so much as the summary expression of an inner process which could not perhaps be made either fully conscious or fully rational. It preserves its own mystery and asks to be met by its hearer in the same spirit. Nietzsche spoke of aphorism as a form which calls on the listener to understand actively and holistically.[2] An elaborated argument might be conceptually irrefragable and yet remain unpersuasive because emptily external. Aphorism, by contrast, gathers up a body of experience and insists on meeting a comparable body of experience in the listener. We have to respond to it in a manner more appropriate to fiction than to argument.

In this respect, the aphoristic tendency of Márquez' characters epitomises the nature of his fiction. It always protects its own meditative space surrounding itself with a distinctive aura for which 'magical realism' is only one, very striking, manifestation. Walter Benjamin once contrasted the traditional story-teller and the novelist to the disadvantage of the latter.[3] The story-teller, he argued, conveys wisdom through a richness of experience which is never brought to a conceptual focus of meaning. By contrast, the novel, which has supplanted story in our culture, requires a conscious organisation of meaning to which no one has a right and which only reveals the uncounselled state of both the novelist and the culture. On this account, the true forebear of the novelist is not Cervantes but his deluded, well-meaning hero, Don Quixote.

Furthermore, I have emphasised throughout that Márquez' fictive self-consciousness is never the controlling frame of significance but only a half-emergent consciousness arising from the realistically objective texture of the narrative and particularly from the language and activity of the characters. This means that instead of the characters becoming merely elements in a fictional game of the author's, the vision engendered by the fiction is implicitly accorded to the characters themselves. Márquez makes us feel this meaning in the characters even if we understand it in a way they do not. This means in turn that the stance defined by the fiction is not ultimately a writerly, but a human, one.

In short, although Márquez, as a writer of fiction, can put the universal condition of solitude to a uniquely creative use, he does so in a way that prevents it being the special privilege of sages, artists and heroes. It is the inner experience of every ethical individual. The anonymous colonel of *No One Writes* is echoed in the world historical figure of Bolívar, who is in turn a secret double of the writer. Márquez' fictional self-consciousness is not self-regarding: it is an emblem of all ethical life. Where Melquíades solitary wisdom in *Hundred Years* suggested a tragic separation of worlds, Márquez' containing narrative, like his fiction at large, shows that solitude may be a necessary condition, and an exemplary form, of solidarity.

Notes

1 Introduction

1. See the selected and annotated bibliography on pp. 155–7.
2. Plinio Apuleyo Mendoza and Gabriel García Márquez *The Fragrance of Guava*, trans. Ann Wright (London: Verso, 1983) pp. 62, 78.
3. For example: Josefina Ludmer, *Cien Años de Soledad: una interpretación* (Buenos Aires, 1972); Michael Palencia-Roth, *Myth and the Modern Novel: Márquez, Mann and Joyce* (New York: Garland, 1987); Robert L. Sims, *The Evolution of Myth in Gabriel García Márquez* (Miami: Universal, 1981).
4. For a good study of the political and historical context of Márquez see Stephen Minta, *Gabriel García Márquez: Writer of Colombia* (London: Cape, 1987).
5. *Philosophical Investigations*, trans. G. E. M. Anscombe (Oxford: Blackwell, 1958) pp. 213–14.
6. *Fragrance*, pp. 53–4.
7. *The Labyrinth of Solitude*, trans. Lysander Kemp (Harmondsworth: Penguin, 1985).
8. In this connection see Miguel de Unamuno's remarks on the cape, with its total isolation within a personal atmosphere, as an expression of the old Castilian character. *En torno al casticismo* (Madrid: Austral, 1943) p. 52. Unamuno's comments on the mixture of free will and fatalism are especially suggestive for the colonel of *No One Writes to the Colonel. En torno* (pp. 75–6).
9. *La ruta de don Quijote*, ed. José Maria Martinez Cachero (Madrid: Catedra, 1988).
10. *Ruta de don Quijote*, p. 114.
11. It is a common observation that the great tradition of Spanish painting is fundamentally indifferent to perspective.
12. For a good modern discussion of this theme see Edwin Williamson, *The Halfway House of Fiction: Don Quixote and Arthurian Romance* (Oxford: Clarendon Press, 1984).

2 Biographical Summary

1. There is actually some uncertainty as to his date of birth which his

147

father believed to be 1927.

2. *Obra Periodistica*, Vol. 2, *Entre Cachacos* I, ed. Jacques Gilard (Barcelona: Bruguera, 1982) pp. 245–62.
3. Ibid., pp. 566–652.
4. *Relato de un naufrago* (Barcelona: Tusquets, 1970).
5. Padilla was detained in 1971 and 'confessed' to incorrect attitudes expressed in his writings. For Maŕquez' own comment, and his difference from his old friend Plinio Apuleyo Mendoza, see *Fragrance*, p. 100. *Index on Censorship* II has a special coverage of the Padilla affair.
6. 'Tuesday Fiesta' appeared in *Los funerales de la Mama Grande* (Xalapa, Mex.: Universidad Veracruzana, 1962). 'The Old Man with Enormous Wings' in *Cuadernos Hispanoamericaños*, No. 245 (Madrid, 1970) 1–6.

3 Journalism and Fiction

1. *Obra Periodistica*, Vol. IV, *De Europa y America*, pp. 763–7.
2. The Spanish 'hojarasca', translated as *Leaf Storm*, means a mass of dead and drifting leaves, hence 'drifters'.
3. Some of his early pieces in *El Heraldo* were stories seeking to create a mysterious atmosphere in a realistic context. 'El Huesped' (The Guest) and 'El Desconocido' (The Stranger) are effectively exercises in this mode. *Obra Periodistica* I, *Textos Costeños*, pp. 308–12.
4. *La Hojarasca* (Buenos Aires: Editorial Sudamericana, 1975) p. 48.
5. *Leaf Storm and Other Stories*, trans. Gregory Rabassa (London: Cape, 1972) p. 32.
6. *L'Étranger* (Paris: Gallimard, 1942). At the end of his remarks on 'the novel of violence' Maŕquez cites Camus as a positive example of the indirect presentation of political violence.
7. This motif is central to Rulfo's novel *Pedro Paramo* (1955) and his collection of stories *The Burning Plain* (1953).
8. *The Labyrinth of Solitude*, p. 191.
9. The references here are to Conrad's *Lord Jim* (1900) and *Heart of Darkness* (1902).
10. The allusion is to Conrad's tale 'The Secret Sharer' (1912).
11. *The Rainbow* (London: Methuen, 1915). Much of Lawrence's poetry was devoted to a meditation on the 'otherness' of non-human life forms.
12. *Obra Periodistica*, Vol. 3, *Entre Cachacos* II, p. 623.
13. *La Hojarasca*, pp. 124, 130; *Leaf Storm*, pp. 90, 95.
14. *El coronel no tiene quien le escriba* (Madrid: Austral, 1986) p. 79.
15. *No One Writes to the Colonel*, trans. J. S. Bernstein (London: Cape, 1971) p. 20.
16. *Obra Periodistica*, Vol. 2, *Entre Cachacos* I, p. 476.
17. *Saving the Appearances: a Study in Idolatry* (New York: Harcourt

Brace, 1965) esp. pp. 45–95.
18. *Othello* was adapted from a novella by Cinthio. The peculiar quality of Hamlet as a 'novelistic' character in a dramatic piece was discussed by Goethe and Schiller and more recently by Barbara Everett in 'Growing' in *The London Review of Books*, 31 March 1988, pp. 6–9.
19. *Fragrance*, p. 62.
20. *Fragrance*, p. 45.
21. *Fragrance*, pp. 47–8.
22. Mr Carmichael is a character in Woolf's *To the Lighthouse*.
23. I give the passage from *Mrs Dalloway* (London: Hogarth Press, 1925) p. 19.
24. *Eichmann in Jerusalem: a Report on the Banality of Evil*, rev. edn (Harmondsworth: Penguin, 1977) esp. pp. 251–2, 287–8.
25. Lieutenant William Calley was convicted in 1971 of a mass killing of the villagers of My-Lai in Vietnam. He was subsequently pardoned by President Nixon.
26. *Obra Periodistica*, Vol. 2, *Entre Cachacos* I, p. 476.
27. *La Mala Hora* (Barcelona: Plaza y Janes, 1974) p. 50. *In Evil Hour*, trans. Gregory Rabassa (London: Cape, 1980) p. 44. Rabassa's 'newspaper talk' for 'literatura de periodico' loses the reference to literature.
28. *Obra Periodistica*, Vol. 3, *Entre Cachacos* II, pp. 910–11.
29. These self-reflexive allusions have, however, been seen in a more patterned, thematic way. See Wolfgang A. Luchting, 'Lampooning Literature', *La mala hora*, in McMurray, pp. 93–102.

4 The Cervantean Turn: *One Hundred Years of Solitude*

1. *Flaubert's Parrot* (London: Cape, 1984).
2. *The Evolution of Mýth in Gabriel García Maŕquez* (Miami: Universal, 1981).
3. *Gabriel García Maŕquez: historia de un deicidio* (Barcelona: Barral, 1981).
4. Prologue to *The Kingdom of this World* (1949).
5. See Gilard's 'Prologo' to *Obra Periodistica*, Vol. 2, *Entre Cachacos* I, p. 70.
6. Jorge Luis Borges, *A Personal Anthology*, ed. Anthony Kerrigan (New York: Grove Press, 1987) pp. 16–23.
7. Andre Breton 'Manifesto of Surrealism' in *Manifestos of Surrealism*, trans. Richard Seaver and Helen R. Lane (University of Michigan Press, 1972) pp. 10–14.
8. *Cien Años de Soledad*, ed. Jacques Joset (Madrid: Catedra, 1987) p. 323.
9. *One Hundred Years of Solitude* (London: Pan, 1978) p. 202.
10. *Illuminations* (London: Fontana, 1973) p. 257.

11. *On the Uses and Disadvantages of History for Life*, trans. Peter Preuss (Indianapolis: Hackett, 1980) p. 10.

12. Jorge Luis Borges, *Labyrinths*, ed. Donald A. Yates and James E. Irby (Harmondsworth: Penguin, 1970) pp. 87–95.

13. *The Birth of Tragedy*, trans. Walter Kaufmann (New York: Vintage, 1967) p. 134.

14. Rama points out that the 'magical' is not peculiar to Latin America, as Carpentier claimed, but to uneducated folk culture, as his example showed. Angel Rama, *Gabriel García Márquez: edificación de un arte nacional y popular* (Universidad de la Republica, Uruguay, 1986) pp. 97–8.

15. *Fragrance*, pp. 114–15.

16. *Fragrance*, p. 106.

17. *Birth of Tragedy*, pp. 68–9.

18. Brian McHale, *Postmodernist Fiction* (London: Routledge, 1989) pp. 134–6.

19. *Metaphors We Live By* (Chicago University Press, 1987).

20. 'It is what human beings *say* that is true and false; and they agree in the *language* they use. That is not agreement in opinions but in form of life.' *Philosophical Investigations*, trans. G. E. M. Anscombe (Oxford: Blackwell, 1958) p. 88.

21. '. . . if a man sees certain human beings as slaves, isn't he . . . rather missing something about himself, or rather something about his connection with these people, his internal relation with them so to speak. When he wants to be served at table by a black hand, he would not be satisfied to be served by a black paw. When he rapes a slave or takes her as a concubine, he does not feel that he has, by that fact itself, embraced sodomy. When he tips a black taxi driver (something he never does with a white driver) it does not occur to him that he might more appropriately have patted the creature fondly on the side of the neck. He does not go to great lengths either to convert his horses to Christianity or to prevent their getting wind of it. Everything in his relation to his slaves shows that he treats them as more or less human – his humiliations of them, his disappointments, his jealousies, his fears, his punishments, his attachments . . . ', *The Claim of Reason* (Oxford: Clarendon Press, 1979) p. 376.

22. 'Prologo' to *Obra periodistica*, 4, *de Europa y America*, pp. 14–15.

23. *Obra Periodistica*, 4, *de Europa y America*, p. 414.

24. Ibid., p. 174.

25. *Labyrinths*, p. 217.

26. *The Labyrinth of Solitude*, p. 161.

27. *Change of Skin*, trans. Sam Hileman (Harmondsworth: Penguin, 1975) p. 263.

28. '. . . it appears likely that poets in our civilization, as it exists at present, must be *difficult*', *Selected Essays* (London: Faber, 1932) p. 289.

29. 'The Waste Land', line 261. *Collected Poems* (London: Faber, 1963) p. 73.
30. *Labyrinths*, p. 219.
31. *On the Uses and Disadvantages of History for Life*, pp. 12–14.
32. *Women in Love*, ed. David Farmer, Lindeth Vasey and John Worthen (Cambridge University Press, 1987) p. 529.
33. *The Rainbow*, ed. Mark Kinkead-Weekes (Cambridge University Press, 1989) p. 258.
34. I discuss Lawrence's narrative hyperbole in *The Rainbow* in *D. H. Lawrence: Language and Being* (Cambridge University Press, 1992) pp. 55–7. The whole chapter on *The Rainbow* provides a fruitful parallel with the present discussion of *Hundred Years*.
35. See my chapter on *The Plumed Serpent* in *D. H. Lawrence: Language and Being*, op. cit., pp. 165–205.
36. Compare Primo Levi's *The Periodic Table* (1975) for a magnificently positive intermingling of story, alchemy and chemistry.
37. *Don Quixote*, trans. Cohen (Harmondsworth: Penguin, 1950) Part II chaps 24–7, pp. 624–51.
38. *The Political Unconscious* (London: Methuen, 1981).
39. I have discussed modernist mythopoeia in 'Myth, Art and Belief' in *Context of English Literature: 1900–30*, ed. Michael Bell (London: Methuen, 1980) pp. 19–43.
40. *Ulysses*, ed. Walter Gabler (Harmondsworth: Penguin, 1986) p. 28.
41. *Labyrinths*, p. 229.
42. Reprinted in *Gabriel García Márquez: New Readings*, ed. B. McGuirk and R. Cardwell (Cambridge University Press, 1987) pp. 207–11.
43. I have discussed the relationship of the curiosity in this story to the curiosity in its narrative context. See 'How Primordial is Narrative?' in *Narrative in Culture*, ed. Cris Nash (London: Routledge, 1990) pp. 172–98.

5   The Magical and the Banal: *The Autumn of the Patriarch*

1. For a recent survey see Gerald Martin, *Journeys through the Labyrinth* (London: Verso, 1989) pp. 237–93.
2. *El otoño del patriarca* (Madrid: Bruguera, 1982) p. 342. *The Autumn of the Patriarch*, trans. Gregory Rabassa (London: Pan, 1978) p. 205.
3. In Kafka's novel, the castle is the centre of mysterious and sinister power.
4. *Idée sur les Romans* (Geneva: Slatkine Reprints, 1967).
5. See Martin, *Journeys*, pp. 271–7.
6. The financier Robert Maxwell committed suicide in 1992, bringing ruin to thousands, particularly in Britain.
7. The regime of Ferdinand Marcos fell in 1986 making way for the election as president of Cory Aquino whose husband had been

assassinated some years before to forestall his likely election victory.

8. *Labyrinth of Solitude*, p. 86.
9. Philip Swanson, *Como leer a Gabriel García Márquez* (Madrid: Jucar, 1991) pp. 131–45.
10. The phrase 'one of us' is a motif of Conrad's *Lord Jim* (1900).
11. *Fragrance*, pp. 86–90.
12. I have discussed this theme at length in *The Sentiment of Reality: Truth of Feeling in the European Novel* (London: Unwin, 1983).
13. 'The Song of the Happy Shepherd', in *The Collected Poems of W. B. Yeats* (London: Macmillan, 1950), pp. 7–8.
14. On this theme see Elizabeth Ermath, *Realism and Consensus in the English Novel* (Princeton University Press, 1983).
15. Amaryllis Chanady makes this her central point in *Magical Realism and the Fantastic* (New York: Garland, 1985).

6 Male Tragedy/Female Novella: *Chronicle of a Death Foretold*

1. *Fragrance*, p. 62.
2. *Cronica de una muerte anunciada* (Bogota, Oveja Negra, 1981) pp. 129–30.
3. *Chronicle of a Death Foretold*, trans. Gregory Rabassa (London: Cape, 1982) p. 100.
4. See Thomas Mann's essay 'Voyage with *Don Quixote*', in *Essays of Three Decades* trans. H. T. Lowe-Porter (London: Secker and Warburg, 1947) pp. 429–64.
5. Barbara M. Jarvis, 'El halcon y la presa: identidades ambiguas en *Cronica de una muerte anunciada*', in *En el punto de mira: Gabriel García Márquez*, ed. Ana Maria Hernandez de Lopez (Madrid: Pliegos, 1985) p. 225.
6. *Don Quixote*, Part II, chaps 64–5, pp. 888–93.
7. *Don Quixote*, Part I, chap. 47. p. 426.
8. *Labyrinths*, pp. 228–31.
9. *A Portrait of the Artist as a Young Man*, ed. Chester G. Anderson and Richard Ellmann (New York: Viking, 1964) p. 204.
10. *Don Quixote*, Part I, chaps 25–6, pp. 199–221.
11. See Murray Krieger, *The Tragic Vision* (New York: Holt Rinehart and Winston, 1960).
12. George Steiner airs this question in *Tolstoy or Dostoevsky* (London: Faber, 1960).
13. Bakhtin saw the novel not so much as a genre in its own right as a form that exists in the assimilation of other genres.
14. For an amplification of this theme see William Rowe, *Rulfo: El llano en llamas* (London: Grant and Cutler, 1987) pp. 31–8.
15. *Doña Perfecta*, Perez Galdos (1876) and *The House of Bernarda Alba* Federico García Lorca (1936). Márquez once remarked on the

frequency of the Bernarda Alba type on the Atlantic coast of Colombia. *Obra Periodistica* 1. *Textos Costeños*, p. 602.

16. On this theme see especially Ruth El Saffar, *Beyond Fiction: the Recovery of the Feminine in the Novels of Cervantes* (Berkeley: University of California Press, 1984).

17. This is the central argument of Bayley's *The Characters of Love* (London: Constable, 1960).

7 Not Flaubert's Parrot: *Love in the Time of Cholera*

1. *El amor en el tiempos del colera* (Barcelona: Bruguera, 1985) p. 100; *Love in the Time of Cholera*, trans. Edith Grossman (London: Cape, 1988) p. 67.

2. Germaine Greer sees Marquez' whole treatment of the theme as 'ageist' although her reading seems humourlessly literalistic to me. See *The Change* (London: Hamish Hamilton, 1991) pp. 364–8.

3. See Denis de Rougemont, *Love in the Western World* (New York: Harper and Row, 1974); also trans. by Montgomery Belgion as *Passion and Society* (London: Faber, 1940).

4. For an extended discussion of this theme see Tony Tanner, *Adultery and the Novel* (Baltimore: Johns Hopkins University Press, 1979).

5. Letter to Alice James, Feb. 22, 1876. *Henry James: Letters*, ed. Leon Edel, Vol. II (London: Macmillan, 1975) pp. 29–30.

6. The published translation gives 'My heart . . . ' but it is clear that Florentino is making a general, aphoristic reflection.

7. Stendhal, *Scarlet and Black*, trans. Margaret R. B. Shaw (Harmondsworth: Penguin, 1953) p. 149.

8. See the interview with Marquez, 'Of Love and Levitation', *TLS*, 20–26 October 1989, pp. 1151–65.

9. See *On Love*, trans. P. Sidney Woolf and C. N. Sidney Woolf (London: Duckworth, 1915). See especially chapter I, sections VI and XII.

10. In a lecture 'García Marquez and the Modernist Tradition' given at a conference on 'Gabriel García Marquez', Birkbeck College, London on 30 September 1988. The interest in popular music of the coastal region is a recurrent feature of Marquez' early journalism. See also Marquez' comment on *Hundred Years* when first working on it: 'It's like a bolero', *Fragrance*, p. 71.

11. 'Pierre Menard, Author of the Quixote', *Labyrinths*, pp. 62–71.

12. I have discussed the relationship of sentimentalist ethics and fictional form in *The Sentiment of Reality* (London: Unwin, 1983).

8 Solitude and Solidarity: *The General in his Labyrinth*

1. *Como leer a García Marquez*, pp. 50–2.

2. *El general en su laberinto* (Madrid: Mondadori, 1989) p. 150.
3. *The General in his Labyrinth*, trans. Edith Grossman (London: Cape, 1991) p. 142.
4. *Uses and Disadvantages of History for Life*, passim.
5. *Collected Poems of W. B. Yeats* (London: Macmillan, 1950) pp. 202–5.
6. Ibid., pp. 142, 391–2.
7. *Labyrinths*, p. 217.

Conclusion

1. The critical discussion on this question is surveyed by Teresa Mendez-Faith in 'Aracataca re-visitada: Genesis y significación de Macondo' in *En el punto de mira: Gabriel García Maŕquez*, pp. 125–35. Mendez-Faith refers in turn to the exhaustive account in Olga Carreras Gonzalez *El mundo de Macondo en la obra de Gabriel García Maŕquez* (Miami: Universal, 1974).
2. See the final paragraph of his Introduction to *The Genealogy of Morals*.
3. *Illuminations*, p. 87.

Select Bibliography

From the vast literature on Marquez and the substantial body of his own writing I have selected items of use to readers approaching his novels in English. After the Fau bibliography, I list his major fictional publications, and some journalism, in English followed by a corresponding list in Spanish including the more important untranslated collections of his journalism. I then list some critical studies in English likely to be most helpful to first-time readers followed by several particularly important discussions in Spanish. The critical list covers a variety of angles and favours recent studies addressing the *œuvre* as a whole.

Bibliography

Fau, Margaret Eustella, *Gabriel García Marquez: an Annotated Bibliography, 1947–1979* (Westport CT: Greenwood Press, 1980).

Fau, Margaret Eustella and Nelly Sfeir de Gonzalez, *Bibliographic Guide to Gabriel García Marquez, 1979–1985* (Westport CT: Greenwood Press, 1986).

Major Works in English in order of Collected Publication

No One Writes to the Colonel and Other Stories, trans. J. S. Bernstein (New York: Harper, 1968).

One Hundred Years of Solitude, trans. Gregory Rabassa (New York: Harper, 1970).

Leaf Storm and other Stories, trans. Gregory Rabassa (New York: Harper, 1972).

The Autumn of the Patriarch, trans. Gregory Rabassa (New York: Harper, 1975).

Innocent Eréndira and Other Stories, trans. Gregory Rabassa (New York: Harper, 1978).

In Evil Hour, trans. Gregory Rabassa (New York: Harper, 1979).

Chronicle of a Death Foretold, trans. Gregory Rabassa (New York: Knopf, 1983).

The Fragrance of the Guava: Plinio Apuleyo Mendoza in conversation with Gabriel García Márquez, trans. Ann Wright (London: Verso, 1983).
The Story of Shipwrecked Sailor, trans. Randolph Hogan (New York: Knopf, 1987).
Clandestine in Chile: the Adventures of Miguel Littin, trans. Asa Zatz (New York: Henry Holt, 1987).
Love in the Time of Cholera, trans. Edith Grossman (New York: Knopf, 1988).
The General in his Labyrinth, trans. Edith Grossman (London: Cape, 1991).

Selected Fiction and Journalism in Spanish

La Hojarasca (Bogota: SLB, 1955).
El coronel no tiene quien le escriba (Medellin: Aguirre, 1961).
La mala hora (Madrid: Luis Perez, 1962). First edition authorised by Márquez (Mexico: Era, 1966).
Los funerales de la Mama Grande (Xalapa, Mex.: Universidad Vera Cruzana, 1962).
Isabel viendo llover en Macondo (Buenos Aires: Estuario, 1967).
Cien Años de Soledad (Buenos Aires: Sudamericana, 1967).
Relato de un naufrago que estuvo diez días a la deriva en una balsa sin comer ni beber, que fue proclamado héroe de la patria, besado por las reinas de la belleza y hecho rico por la publicidad, y luego aborrecido por el gobierno y olvidado para siempre (Barcelona: Tusquets, 1970).
Ojos de perro azul; nueve cuentos desconocidos (Rosario, Argen.: Equiseditorial, 1971).
La increíble y triste historia de la cándida Eréndira y de su abuela desalmada (Barcelona: Barral, 1972).
El otoño del patriarca (Barcelona: Plaza y Janes, 1975).
García Márquez habla de Garcia Márquez (Bogota: Renteria, 1979).
Crónica de una muerte anunciada (Bogota: Oveja Negra, 1981).
De viaje por los paises socialistas: 90 dias en la 'Cortina de Hierro' (Bogota: Oveja Negra, 1981).
Obra Periodistica, ed. Jacques Gilard (Barcelona: Bruguera, 1982) in four volumes: *Textos costeños*; *Entre cachacos I*; *Entre cachacos II*, *De Europa y America*.
El olor de ia guayaba: Conversacion con Plinio Apuleyo Mendoza (Barcelona: Bruguera, 1982).
El amor en los tiempos del cólera (Bogota: Oveja Negra, 1985).
La aventura de Miguel Littin clandestino in Chile (Madrid: El Pais, 1986).
El general en su laberinto (Madrid: Mondadori, 1989).
Doce cuentos peregrinos (Madrid: Mondadori, 1992).

Selected Criticism in English

Bell-Villada, Gene H., *Gabriel García Márquez: the Man and his Work* (University of California Press, 1990). A generously informative survey for an English-speaking readership by a Latin American.

Martin, Gerald, *Journeys through the Labyrinth* (London: Verso, 1989). An extensive study of Latin American fiction touching substantially on Márquez, albeit at times from a reductively political angle.

McGuirk, Bernard and Richard Cardwell (eds), *Gabriel García Márquez: New Readings* (Cambridge University Press, 1987). Includes Márquez' Nobel prize acceptance speech and some good essays, most notably Edwin Williamson on *Hundred Years*.

McMurray, George R. (ed.), *Critical Essays on Gabriel García Márquez*. (Boston: Hall, 1987) Collects early reviews with essays on individual works. Includes Ricardo Gullon's 'Gabriel García Márquez and the Lost Art of Storytelling' otherwise available as a separate volume in Spanish.

Minta, Stephen, *Gabriel García Márquez: Writer of Columbia*, An excellent reading of Márquez in his national historical context.

Ortega, Julio (ed.), *Gabriel García Márquez and the Powers of Fiction* (Austin: University of Texas Press, 1988). Several of these essays are too finely spun but they offer recent alternative treatment of themes covered in the present study.

Sims, Robert L., *The Evolution of Myth in Gabriel García Márquez* (Miami: Ediciones Universal, 1981). A close analysis of narrative time if rather narrow in its conception of myth.

Wood, Michael, *Gabriel García Márquez: One Hundred Years of Solitude* (Cambridge University Press, 1990). Although focused on one novel, this is an accessible and suggestive discussion of Márquez generally.

Criticism in Spanish

Earle, Peter G. (ed.), *Gabriel García Márquez* (Madrid: Taurus, 1981). A packed collection of essays by many of the best known critics on Márquez.

Farias, Victor, *Los Manuscritos de Melquíades* (Frankfurt: Klaus Dieter Vervuert Verlag, 1981). A close Marxist reading of historical process in *Hundred Years*.

Ludmer, Josefina, *Cien Años de Soledad: una interpretación* (Buenos Aires, Editorial Tiempo Contemporaneo, 1972). Reveals the intricacy of symbolic structure in *Hundred Years*.

Maturo, Graciela, *Claves Simbólicas de Gabriel García Márquez* (Buenos Aires: Cambiero, 1972). Mainly devoted to an alchemical reading of *Hundred Years*. Useful even if losing the literary wood in the symbolic trees.

Rama, Angel, *Gabriel García Márquez; edificación de una arte nacional y popular* (Uruguay, Universidad de la Republica, 1986). The doyen of Latin American criticism reflects on the cultural historical significance of Márquez.

Vargas Llosa, Mario, *Gabriel García Márquez: historia de un deicidio* (Barcelona: Barral, 1971). A little long and over-thorough, but full of telling insights arising from personal friendship and from the understanding of a fellow novelist.

Index